T0128570

Looking for Him in All the Right Places

Revised Edition

Jim Hall

WestBow Press books may be ordered through booksellers or by contacting:

WestBow Press
A Division of Thomas Nelson & Zondervan
1663 Liberty Drive
Bloomington, IN 47403
www.westbowpress.com
844-714-3454

ISBN: 978-1-9736-8026-0 (sc)
ISBN: 978-1-9736-8027-7 (hc)
ISBN: 978-1-9736-8025-3 (e)

Library of Congress Control Number: 2019919698

Print information available on the last page.

WestBow Press rev. date: 11/12/2020

Ask and it will be given to you; seek and you will find; knock and the door will be opened to you. For everyone who asks receives; the one who seeks finds; and to the one who knocks, the door will be opened.

—Matthew 7:7–8

Contents

This book is dedicated to my wife Marsha and to my children Molly, Wendy, David and Annie.

To my friends and counselors in the Christian Business Men's Connection (CBMC): Dave Waterman, John Burdis, Gene Latta, Gary Henson, Gerry Richardson, Bill Bartholomew, Dave Buch, Fred Baber, Jamie Mladenoff, Tony Beckett, and in loving memory of Bill Michael.

To Pastors Bob Penton, Robbins Sims, Dennis Keller, Tom Jacobs, Brendan Hock, Greg Rapp, Joshua Rhone, Larry Katz, and in loving memory of Pastors Tom Cartwright and Bill Garrett.

To the Library Class of First United Methodist Church, Hanover, Pennsylvania.

To the Covenant Brothers: Dale Gordon, Steve Bortner, Steve Miller, Steve Strevig, Sterling Hoffmaster, Kent Hoffmaster, Gordon Fisher, Chuck Fereday, Fred Baber, Tom Henry, Larry Jackson, Craig Minetola, Bill Ingram and in loving memory of Ralph Ruggles.

To my friends and valued workmates Jim Tavenner, Anna Bender, and Loni Burdis Smith.

Preface

Here is what this book is about:

- It's about making decisions and committing to them. Life is the sum of the large and small decisions we make on an everyday basis. We need to be conscious, aware, and intentional about them.
- It's about objectivity. Objectivity is about reality versus fantasy, about true versus false. We should know when we are being objective and when we aren't.
- It's about language: knowing and being able to articulate what our words mean.
- It's about God and religion.
- It's about the search for God, and about conducting that search in a systematic manner.
- It's about modern culture and technology.
- It's about values and meaning.
- It's about the Bible.
- It's about consciousness and the role God plays in it.
- It's about the Apostle Paul, a primary founder of the Christian faith.
- It's about Jesus of Nazareth, Emmanuel, or "God with us."

Chapter One

Did You Ever Have to Finally Decide?

> If I would preserve my relation to nature, I must make my life more moral, more pure and innocent. The problem is so precise and simple as a mathematical one. I must not live loosely, but more and more continently [deliberately].[1]
>
> —Henry David Thoreau

Essentials

Henry David Thoreau was a mid-19th century thinker, philosopher and writer who lived in and near Concord, Massachusetts. His basic philosophy came to be known as Transcendentalism, and its adherents included Thoreau's friend, mentor and benefactor Ralph Waldo Emerson, and a somewhat lesser light, Bronson Alcott (Bronson was the father of Louisa May Alcott, author of *Little Women*). Essentially the Transcendentalists believed that the divinity (God) pervaded all of nature, and, if we are to draw close to Him, then we must seek Him there—and pay close attention.

To augment his search—indeed to be fully steeped in it—Thoreau decided to build and occupy a small cabin near Walden Pond, close to Concord. In doing so, he unwittingly anticipated our tiny house movement here in twenty-first-century America. His cabin, which he built himself, was ten feet by fifteen feet; it consisted of one room having one door. He did most of the building himself, including procuring needed materials and chopping down the trees needed for the roof and walls. He wanted to simplify his life to the greatest extent possible; as he said—

> I went to the woods because I wished to live deliberately, to front only the essential facts of life, and see if I could not learn what it had to teach, and not, when I came to die, discover that I had not lived.[2]

If Thoreau really wanted to "rough it," one would think he'd have chosen a spot more than a mile-and-a-half from downtown Concord—but, he didn't. Still, a mile-and-a-half or a thousand miles distant from "civilization," his thoughts and experiences have exerted a tremendous influence. One of my ideas in this book is that perhaps we too should live more deliberately than we do.

Earthly life has a definite beginning and a definite end. We don't know how much of it we'll have, so Thoreau's idea about "spending" our allotted hours and days deliberately does make sense.

This is the idea that Thoreau homes in on. Time is precious, so he wants to spend his wisely—not "loosely" or incontinently. To provide an illustration, we can apply this idea to being aboard a plane that crashes in the desert. Survivors have an extremely limited amount of water. They don't know how long that water will have to last. Their problem indeed is as "precise and simple as a mathematical one." Until they can be sure of rescue, they need to make sure their precious water lasts.

Water is what the survivors "invest" in as a guarantee of survival. When we invest, we attribute value to something, and then we deploy methods and assets to preserve or acquire it. We read to acquire wisdom. We exercise to build health. We travel to learn about other places and people. Time is the most valuable asset we have. Money does us no good if we lack the minutes and hours to spend it! And ironically, time is also the asset that we may be the most careless about. It makes sense that we invest our time deliberately, in ways that will yield the greatest return to us and those close to us.

I want you to think seriously about what is essential in *your* life. I want you to think about what you're investing yourself in today (e.g., education, work, model train layout, alcohol, stamp collection, relationships, food, video games, children, exercise, and body art) and think about these investments in terms of risk and reward (and also the minutes, hours and days you dedicate to them). Investment advisors like to talk about diversifying their clients' portfolios to spread risk and to have eggs strategically placed in several baskets. We'll be talking about a basket that may need more eggs than you're currently putting into it.

There's a stirring scene in the Academy Award-winning film *Gladiator* in which the main character speaks of the impact of the present on the future. Russell Crowe plays Maximus, a general in the Roman army who's about to lead cavalry into battle against a Germanic tribe. He addresses his men before they move out. He raises his sword and shouts, "What we do in life, echoes in eternity!" He is saying that we reap what we sow. We need to sow carefully now if we're to reap bountifully later.

What we do now, today, affects the harvest of tomorrow.

Investing Wisely

In reading Thoreau, we learn that God for him is a central reality, one of the "essential facts of life." Thoreau wanted to be out there in the woods, by himself, where he wouldn't be distracted by things he deemed frivolous, unreal, and having little lasting value.

Let me share with you some assumptions and definitions. We have to start with an idea of Who God is. I will ask you to think carefully about God, so I think it only fair to give us a starting place—my own idea of Who He is.

In Judeo-Christian scripture (the Bible), God is the entity who created "the heavens and the earth." This means the universe. He is a spiritual force, not an elderly person with a beard seated on a cloud, lyre (harp) close at hand. Christians believe that since God's created people kept refusing to get His message and live as He intended, that He chose to be born on earth, to show us through His earthly life, death, and resurrection from the dead that He is indeed real, that He continues to oversee the affairs of human kind. His human, earthly name was Jesus of Nazareth; he was the child of Joseph and Mary, and His family lived not far from the Sea of Galilee in Roman-occupied Palestine. When a disciple asked Jesus at one point to be shown the Father, Jesus said that if he'd seen Him (Jesus), then he'd seen the Father.

God is said to be a "triune" (three part) entity: Father, Son and Holy Ghost (Spirit). The latter exists as the unseen "Helper" that Jesus promised his disciples (to be with them after Jesus's ascension into heaven).

With this brief background, let's acknowledge that, indeed, today, God may not be as central to many people as He was formerly. By "central," I mean a subject that occupies a good deal of our attention, our time, our interest, and our investment of energy—to say nothing of our love and gratitude. We are all subject to (and in many cases enthralled by) many distractions. We are often captivated by the media that transmit these distractions to us, via smartphones, laptops, iPads, and wall-sized television screens. We appear to need the clearest, fastest, most durable, and most flexible of these devices.

Let me acknowledge too, here at the outset, that I am no shining example of one who always allows God first place in my life. Beyond the fact that we are all sinners, all falling short of living the lives God would have us live, I am, with the Apostle Paul (much more about him later) among the worst of sinners.

I get as distracted as anyone. For myself, and many of us, it could be time to take another look at what we are, indeed, invested in, and at what the payoff of these investments is likely to be in terms of peace of mind, physical and emotional health, life span, and ultimate value. I do suggest adding God to our investment portfolios. If He's already there (in your portfolio), I suggest increasing the proportion of the investments you allot to Him.

We do live at breakneck speed, and in an increasing tide of information, although much of it is misinformation, and a lot of it is unhealthy. We can, however, change what we pay attention to, the way we live and the environments we choose to live in. Change is possible; it's possible to clear space in your mind and heart and choose other options when necessary. It may be time to make an important decision regarding your investment choices. I can give you a couple of examples from my own experience.

Some History

On January 31, 1982, I decided that I'd had enough to drink. Not water, understand, but alcohol.

Starting in my mid-teens, I invested a solid couple of decades as a consumer of alcohol, but decided in early 1982 that I'd had enough. Many who knew me before that date might not have perceived the hold alcohol had on me, but I came to see it. I could see that this investment was wrongheaded, that the returns I received were not in proportion to the harm being caused.

Those who alter their consciousness through alcohol or drugs live at least a dual nature, if not a many-sided one. They live in constant tension between the two states: either under the influence or out of it. I was helped to see that investing my time, treasure, and health in the activity of drinking was not going to yield rewarding returns in life, and that it would be a good idea to drop it from my investment mix. So I did, thirty-seven years ago—not a drop of alcohol to drink since that time.

To cite a second example, on August 28, 1986, I decided that I wanted to marry Marsha Maxfield. She decided that she wanted to marry me as well. Marsha and I had been best friends for three years and worked for the same company. We went to the courthouse in Birmingham, Alabama one day on our lunch break to pick up the last of the required paperwork. Somehow, the necessary documents and people would not be available later in the week when we'd planned to marry, but they were available at that moment.

So we made a decision: "Well, we're here. Let's do this." So we did. We decided to invest in one another and get married. We'd both looked at how life was without the other and decided that life together would be better. This happened thirty-three years ago.

When we got married, I promised Marsha that I would always be faithful to her. She made that same promise to me, and she also promised to be nice to me. We've been faithful and nice to each other now for a long time.

Change is possible. A better, more focused life is possible.

The poet Robert Frost makes the following point in the last verse of "Two Roads Diverged in a Yellow Wood":

> I shall be telling this with a sigh
> Somewhere ages and ages hence:
> Two roads diverged in a wood, and I—
> I took the one less traveled by,
> And that has made all the difference.

Frost says he "*took* [emphasis mine] the one less traveled by." What he means is that he *chose* the one less traveled by. He made a decision to opt for one direction over another.

I know that it's difficult to make decisions in our media-centric, news-around-the-clock culture. As my drinking and marriage examples show, to live well and arrive at a meaningful destination in life, we really do have to finally decide some things. We need to look seriously at the pluses and minuses of the way we're living. We need to see if we can add some things to that first column and subtract some things from the second.

The Anatomy of Decisions

Don't let me suggest that this changing directions business is easy. If it were, we'd all be healthier, wealthier, and wiser. This applies especially to addictions—to alcohol, opioids, the gym, our appearance, sex, food, and so forth. It's not a simple matter for addicts to just decide to move in another direction. Other resources often have to be sought to bolster the commitment to live another way, but the essential step in the whole process is making that initial decision. Without that, prospects for changing something for the better diminish considerably.

As we contemplate change, we do need to realize that we are pretty heavily invested already. Whatever's in our portfolios can exert a powerful hold on us every day. Long-held habits exert something like a gravitational pull, tugging us along paths of least resistance—they become ruts that are hard to climb out of. As I write this, a Sausage Egg McMuffin is calling me urgently from *its* well-traveled rut. With some effort I can hop out of that rut—maybe opt for some granola instead. What's that saying? Something like "A journey of a thousand miles begins with a single step"? Unless you're willing to take that first step, there won't be a new journey. It's possible, though. We can evaluate where we are and make a commitment to a better way. A more "continent" way, as Thoreau says.

You're not being asked for a final decision now, you realize; you're simply being asked to consider something that may have escaped your focused, dedicated attention.

Eventually though, understand that decisions without *commitment* are worthless. Thoreau's decision to build that cabin and live in it required more than a whim. Commitment involves dedication; it moves something from the realm of promise to the hard work of day-to-day reality. Decisions also involve patience. Wise financial investors know that they can't time the markets. They know that they need to decide on a rational selection of different financial instruments and then stick with them over time, allowing enough time for valley periods to be adjusted by peak periods.

Committed decisions also involve some risk. Whatever behaviors that formerly enabled us to move from Point A to Point B in life—e.g., having a few drinks to settle our nerves—will no longer be available. Something else will have to settle our nerves.

Deciding to realize the rewards of a loving relationship for a lifetime with one person involves the risk of *not* being in a relationship with any number of other people. In relationships, as in everything else, it's perhaps wise to at least consider the risk/reward equation before heading down a particular path.

The Whole God Thing

"The Whole God Thing" is how some refer to considerations involving God. I sense some skepticism in referring to God this way.

If you are skeptical, you may take some comfort in knowing that you have company. Many of us can't let go of what we perceive the "reins" of our lives to be. *We* want to be God! If we acknowledge the Genuine Article, then *we* have to let go! Terrifying! Should you have this thought, I would simply pose the question, "How are things working for you?" Rather than trying to figure a lot of things out on our own (and acting on them), Jesus of Nazareth (Emmanuel or "God with us") invites us to become "yoked" with Him. Let Him lead. We can help *pull*, but He asks us to let Him lead.

You may well ask why else we should increase our awareness of, correspondence with, and reliance on the Creator of the Universe.

Beyond the fact that many of us bungle the job in epic fashion, we can study the power of God, and what it has taken to set this whole thing (the universe) in motion.

Dallas Willard in *Renovation of the Heart* asks us to remember this, to keep in mind the "power" question. He says that "God is not mean, but he is dangerous. It is the same with other great forces he has placed in reality. Electricity and nuclear power are not mean, but they are dangerous."[3] We will have more to say about this point in later chapters.

Jonathan Edwards was a fire and brimstone preacher of the eighteenth century, who preached a sermon called "Sinners in the Hands of an Angry God." He introduces us to the devil, Satan, the anti-God who rebelled against the power and authority of God. An image Edwards chooses is that each of us—at least those of us reluctant to change our ways—are suspended by Satan, who holds us by the slenderest of threads over the fiery pit of hell. It's only due to God's love and patience that Satan doesn't release the thread and allow us to fall in. Yes, we will have more to say about this least desirable of destinations—hell—later.

To continue our portfolio metaphor, we can also place our investment choices in the context of risk and reward, cause and effect. Our investments—of time, treasure, physical exertion, emotion, intellect—may not be yielding the return we expected. We sense that we're missing something, and fear can emerge that our time to find something else is diminishing (remember those plane crash victims, who had a limited amount of water).

The wise course is to consider investing in something real and lasting. It can be unwise to wait, allowing God to become the investment of last resort, a solution that we discover only after discovering how far short other solutions fall. We often need to accumulate a number of years before we even ask the question, to say nothing of living out the answer to the question in a meaningful way.

Any investment should be preceded by investigation and research. It can be ill-advised to engage in anything without doing what can be called due diligence: doing our homework, acquiring information. While God's story is set forth in the Bible, it can be daunting to sit down after dinner of a particular evening and say, "I'm going to read this." So I'll try to provide some very basic information about the Bible that I hope will be helpful.

To the Rescue

As we discussed earlier, God chose to appear in earthly form in ancient Palestine as Jesus of Nazareth, child of Joseph and Mary. He had to show in Person what He'd already covered in scripture. An early Robert Redford film, *Brubaker,* is based on this principle: to better understand conditions in a prison, Redford as a new warden allows himself to be processed in as a prisoner. From that perspective, he's able to facilitate meaningful change. God literally imprisoned *Himself* in a human body to achieve the human versus the Creator of the Universe perspective.

Of God becoming human, Thoreau suggests that this would be like one of us becoming an ant, the better to show the other ants in the hill how to be—how to be what they were created to be. God made the decision to enter time and space as a tiny, helpless baby. He went on to live the life and communicate the ideas that he wanted His people to adopt. The ideas and methods of His early church came to be called "the Way."

The "way" that Jesus describes is one that many find worthy of investing in and committing to. You see from the foregoing that people can be pursuing a given path, and that they can choose to step onto another path. Not only can they identify such a path; they can also make and sustain a commitment to staying on it. To use our other metaphor, they can look at their investment portfolios, make some adjustments, and hope for a higher rate of return.

Life by Default

Sometimes, we really hurt ourselves by failing to decide and making a commitment to another way of being. There's a thought-provoking short story by Henry James called "The Beast in the Jungle." The main character in that story, John Marcher, believes that his life is destined to end in some catastrophic way—perhaps with a safe falling on him. The "beast in the jungle" is this horrific event he imagines will befall him.

He is acquainted with a wonderful woman named May Bartram. We see right away that he should marry May and live happily ever after. But no. Since he has this idea that the beast is going to get him, he thinks it unfair to marry and subject a wife to the unbearable loss of him—which will apparently happen suddenly when the safe falls on him. This idea may not qualify as *total* idiocy, but it's well within range.

Marcher and May never get together. She eventually dies. Marcher comes to understand that the real beast in the jungle is his own ill-conceived idea that something horrible would happen to him.

If we compare this to a hand of poker, Marcher went "all in" too soon—bet everything before he had to. Once he made that bet, made that decision, the rest of his life aligned itself accordingly. He was unable or unwilling to see other good possibilities for himself, one of which was the lovely Ms. Bartram and the life they could have had together.

We can commit on the basis of too little and the wrong kind of data, and this can make all the difference.

The Important Decisions

It's best to make conscious decisions about life's major components, rather than leaving them to time, destiny, chance, or whim. Don't pledge the "Just Do It" fraternity. We will say more in later chapters about distractions, about how difficult it is for us in the technological age to focus and pay attention. For now, we'll say simply that John Marcher got hurt through his failure to decide. Failure to decide about God could be a similar beast in the jungle.

In fact, the decision about God may well be a life-and-death matter. For some, the idea of life after death is at the core of their decision to believe in God or not. Let me tell you one quick life-after-death story.

On January 18, 1989, Don Piper, an ordained minister who lived in Texas, was killed in a car accident. His compact car was crushed by a truck that hit him head on, squashing his car into a concrete guardrail. Paramedics could find no pulse and covered both Piper and his car with a canvas tarp, before tending to other details at the crash scene.

Piper was dead for ninety minutes. Dick Onerecker, a minister who'd been with Piper at a conference shortly before the accident, came upon the accident scene shortly after it happened. Unable to open the doors, he crawled in through the back of the car, put his hand on Piper's lifeless body, and began to pray for him.

Here is Piper's account of what happened next:

> Dick knew I was dead. Not only had the police officer told him but he also had checked for a pulse. He had no idea why he prayed as he did, except God told him to. He didn't pray for the injuries he could see, only for the healing of internal damage. He said he prayed the most passionate, fervent, emotional prayer of his life. As I would later learn, Dick was a highly emotional man anyway.
>
> Then he began to sing again. "O what peace we often forfeit, O what needless pain we bear, all because we do not carry everything to God in prayer!" The only

> thing I personally know for certain about the entire event is that as he sang the blessed old hymn "What a Friend We Have in Jesus," I began to sing with him.[4]

Piper was dead and came back to life. After he was killed, he went to heaven—spending ninety minutes after his earthly death there. The description of heaven and the description of Piper's long and difficult recovery from his injuries occupy the rest of his book.

Was Piper truly dead? Did his spirit really ascend to and return from heaven? The evidence is persuasive that he was and that he did.

Rather than certainties, we deal more often with probabilities, based on the quality and kind of evidence we have. We look at the performance of the assets we include in our portfolios. We make judgments as to the likelihood or improbability of a given report or phenomenon. Do writers and reporters make a documented, carefully qualified assertion, or are they given to wild hyperbole (exaggeration). These are questions we can ask of everyone we read or listen to. They will come into play later as we listen carefully to biblical writers such as Luke and Paul.

Don Piper's story is one that suggests that a life with God, which carries with it the promise of eternal life, is something for us to think about.

In addition to what we read and hear, we also come to believe certain ways and in certain things because of our tangible experience with them. What Don Piper perceived as direct experience with heaven obviously had a marked effect on him. Other times, we come to believe something because of what others have told us about it, applying some of the evaluative criteria mentioned above. We can come to believe something based on someone else's authority and because of the weight of other evidence that's out there.

Change

I don't know where you're looking for satisfaction and fulfillment, what you've invested your life in to this point. Maybe we never achieve those states (satisfaction and fulfillment) to the degree that we'd like. But experience teaches that we can be more satisfied, more at peace with ourselves, with other people, and with life in general. First, though, we need to discover what it is about our approach to life that may not be working as well as we'd like it to.

Can we speak briefly of what some common places are that people search for meaning in life? We can use this as our starter list:

- wealth
- possessions
- power
- freedom
- appearance
- love
- relationships
- model trains
- body art
- success
- sports
- exercise
- the Chicago Bears
- happiness
- accomplishment
- prestige
- position
- diversion
- approval

Perhaps I don't even have to parse through this list. We know at some level that pursuit of one or more of the areas listed rarely if ever provides a final answer to our search for meaning and satisfaction. Let's look at just a few.

Wealth? The Beatles may have had something when they sang, "I don't care too much for money—money can't buy me love." Indeed it can't; perhaps it can rent a facsimile of it for a time, but it can't buy the genuine article.

Diversion? Consider what we choose to be diverted *from*. We often work for a year to earn a vacation, a diversion from our usual routine. Vacations end; not a reliable place to look for genuine, *ongoing* satisfaction. Battery charging certainly; source of peace and satisfaction, not so much. Video games as diversion? Going back to Super Mario, I never had the least bit of success with video games, so I'm going to disqualify myself.

Approval? Certainly nice to have, but not something that can be reliably built upon. We win one person's or group's approval, and perhaps earn scorn and derision from another person or another group. Approval from others is too often shifting and brief, the criteria needed to obtain it unclear.

Love? Now here we have some currency. But we need to be clear about what we mean by love, and from whom we seek to find it.

I add God to our list, remembering that God in human form, Jesus Christ, said that He is the way, the truth, and the life.

We can become addicted to the items on this list. Exercise, for example, wealth, or a sports team. When this happens, we assign importance that is disproportionate to the potential value we receive—in terms of the essentials we discussed at the beginning of this chapter.

The Current Milieu

Let me say briefly how exponentially more difficult it is to finally decide and commit in our current, social media-dominated culture (this is what "milieu" refers to). Perhaps never have so many had the ability to say so little of consequence to so many. In earlier times, children were to be seen, not heard. Now they have their own social media platforms (platforms plural).

Other distractions:

- In our vehicles, we can't attend to the task at hand (driving) without keeping one if not both eyes on our phones. Our attention spans tend to be brief, and what we do focus on can be trivial and short-lived.

- Our personal random access memory (RAM) can only handle so much data, and it is often inundated with fragmentary perceptions, incomplete impressions, and superficial judgments. If we tune into it, news bombards us 24/7. News can be fake or legitimate.
- We are consumed by an often feverish need to acquire and implement the newest and fastest ways to inject data into ourselves—into our already-overloaded processing systems. We can't make good sense of data already swirling around in our brains but feel the need to add more,

In this environment, how do we envision and then live out even quality moments, let alone meaningful lives? How many of us pause to consider where we'll eventually end up and what things will be like when we get there? What conclusions will we be able to draw as to what our lives have meant? This is what Thoreau wanted to "front" in his life at Walden Pond.

Finding meaning and purpose—things intrinsically valuable and worthy of our commitment—certainly used to be easier. Marriages lasted longer. Politicians spoke to each other and even cooperated on certain issues. Children went outside to play. If people wanted to talk with you on the phone, they called you at your home number. If you weren't home, you didn't get the call. You could be phone-free just by walking outside.

To quite a degree, life was *slower.* We could take deep breaths and pay attention. We could think things through. It was easier for us to take the time we needed to make good decisions and commit to them. We had more of an opportunity, if we chose, to decide on a life path and then follow it. We could often consider life's most serious questions and come to reasonable conclusions about how to answer them.

Quality answers to these serious questions lie in our ability to pause, to think, to plan, to decide, to commit, and then to invest. Given the environment we find ourselves in, it will be helpful to look at that last component in particular detail.

Life lived frantically, in the vast majority of cases, can be neither satisfying nor productive. These qualities require the ability to stop and think. The decision (and the ability) to either stop the high-speed train we're on or jump off of it needs our careful attention. I lean in the direction of jumping.

A life is a culmination of discrete, separate decisions and commitments. We can ask ourselves if we even have that capacity any more. This book uses one important area of life (spirituality and our perceived relationship to God) to explore our ability to live more meaningfully. To live, as Thoreau said earlier, perhaps "more continently" than we are.

To summarize:

- We may not realize all the time that what we're doing is a product of a decision (e.g., subsequent drinking behavior follows an initial decision to drink alcohol).
- We can examine our lives, see what course we're on, and choose a different course.
- We can paralyze ourselves (like John Marcher) and live life according to a default position.
- The decision toward God or away from Him is one we should make consciously, rather than leaving it to chance.
- We can research decisions or rely primarily on our experience.
- Our culture makes our task (making decisions in a calm and rational manner) more difficult but not impossible.

We don't approach decisions concerning God with a blank slate. Our thoughts and feelings have been shaped by everything in our lives that has happened to us. This has given us some baggage—some of it quite heavy.

As we'll see in the next chapter, it may be time to unpack, repack, or just start all over.

Chapter Two

Baggage Check

It is never too late to give up your prejudices. No way of thinking or doing, however ancient, can be trusted without proof.[5]
—Henry David Thoreau

Prejudice means "judging before the fact." It means making up our minds before all the evidence is in. Thoreau says that we all have prejudices, and he's right.

In this book, when I use what may be an unfamiliar term (such as "hyperbole" in the first chapter), I offer my definition of what that word means. This is so you can't accuse me of not knowing what I'm talking about. My definition may not be the same as yours, but at least I share with you what it is.

When people can't or don't do this, we can accurately determine that they don't, in fact, know what they're talking about. Or they may, and they just haven't shared that with us yet.

Semanticists, those who study language and meaning, sometimes refer to words and definitions as maps and territories, respectively. When we say "Wyoming," we refer to a state in the United States that occupies a very definite territory. Communication is possible when people ensure that they are clear about which territory they are mapping with the use of a particular word.

These same semanticists talk about something called the "abstraction ladder." An abstraction is also a map, in that it stands for something else. When we talk about something being high up on an abstraction ladder, we mean that it can have a variety of different territories or definitions. "Transportation" is very abstract. "The blue 2016 Nissan Sentra sitting in my garage" is very concrete.

Thoreau, in his comment above about prejudices, wants us to be clear about the words and definitions that we live by. If we aren't, then we can be living according to ideas that have little correlation to reality. As this is written, some in the political realm speak of "fake news," without always clarifying what they mean by that.

Many of us have strange definitions rattling around in our heads. If we don't get out much and don't share those definitions with people, the definitions can become hardened and fixed in place, as can the emotions associated with them. For example, what territory comes to mind when you hear the word "liberal"? "Conservative"? Unless we frequently engage in the practice of supplying maps/definitions for people (and ourselves), we are communicating very little.

A linguistically and intellectually more satisfying approach is to be clear about our words and their definitions. Every day, we are formulating and acting out a philosophy of life, trying to live as honestly, ethically, and responsibly as we can. It's through our words and sentences that others interpret how we're doing.

The Past as Present

It's in the details of our experience as a whole that our general outlook on life has marinated or percolated, sometimes becoming quite a strange brew, one whose origins may be largely unknown. For many of us, it may have been percolating for so long that we have lost track of what its ingredients are. We're not clear as to why we believe as we do.

This lack of clarity leads us to take a lot of our beliefs and the behaviors associated with them for granted. We may have forgotten why we believe, talk and act as we do. We can find it difficult to recall particular books, friendships, relationships, accidents, lessons and conversations—and say "Aha! That's where that idea came from!"

To insert myself into the equation, however they got there, my beliefs or prejudices reside in my consciousness, ready to assert themselves, ready to influence me for good or ill in any given moment. I hope the reality I experience daily conforms in some fashion to the one in my head (i.e., I hope territories still match the maps I have of them). When external reality doesn't match up well to our own private one, we say that we are out of sync with the world around us and with the ideas that populate it.

I think of "gerrymandering" in this context. Gerrymandering occurs when those in political power redraw voting districts in ways that benefit their particular political party. Regardless of what a literal map may reflect in a given geographic area, a redistricted map comes to reflect the desired *political* map of those in authority. We don't want to do this with our mental and spiritual maps. We want our maps to reflect an honest, accurate reflection of the world as it is.

Our consciousness is not unlike GPS. The GPS operating in our vehicle guides us in the direction we want to go. (Full disclosure: I don't like, nor do I use, the GPS in my vehicle.) Theoretically, GPS doesn't let us go far astray. If it says Maple Street is coming up in .6 mile, well then, we can look out the windshield and see this with our own eyes. We check what we've been told is coming with what we actually see.

Our conscious and unconscious minds (call them our internal guidance systems) are influenced if not actually somewhat programmed by everything that's happened to us up to the present moment. They may resemble NASA's Mission Control—a collection of connected data points that we hope keep us in a particular orbit.

A GPS or mission control center is useful only to the degree that its information is correct. If either transmits incorrect information, people end up in the wrong places. You've heard the phrase "garbage in, garbage out." Inaccurate or wrong information is garbage, in the sense that it's not achieving its purpose—which, again, is all about guiding things toward desired destinations. To apply this to us, if our awareness is too badly skewed—however the skewing may have occurred—then we may be flying blind. We risk going into orbit around the wrong planet or ending up in Duluth when we wanted to go to Oshkosh.

Data Processing

Select the metaphor from above that makes the most sense to you (GPS, stew, mission control). In using those analogies, I'm trying to make the point that however it happens, we are *guided*. Something in our consciousness is saying, "Do this or do that; go here or go there; believe this or believe that." It seems best to me that we know as clearly as we can why we perceive, think, believe, and act as we do. If we don't or can't, as Thoreau says, we are acting out of prejudice.

Apparently, everything we ever perceive goes into our memory banks and never leaves. In this way, the facts of our experience are always with us, as are the feelings associated with them. We do our processing in the moment something occurs and also archive events to be recalled and responded to at a later time. Have you had *déjà vu*? In these moments, we could swear that an experience we're in the midst of has happened before (and perhaps it has).

Sometimes, the weight from the past can be heavy, the memory banks filled with painful, even tragic things we've been through. Think of Eeyore in the Winnie the Pooh stories. I don't know if we ever learn the reasons why Eeyore is overwhelmingly sad, but something is definitely weighing him down. A way to say this is that Eeyore carries a lot of baggage with him.

The weight in our conscious memories of people and events is accompanied by the feelings generated by those people and events. A recent film directed by Robert Zemeckis, called *Welcome to Marwen,* offers an example of what I mean. In the film, which is based on a true story, a man suffers a terrible beating and afterward is affected by post-traumatic stress disorder. To escape the memory of the beating, the main character creates what amounts to another reality, a fictional village. Again, I think it better to live in real villages rather than fictional ones.

We need to be aware of the history we bring to life events, as well as that carried by those around us. Sometimes, one dramatic, perhaps traumatizing event stamps us in a certain way—as in the Marwen example just cited.

Frame of Reference

The totality of our past experience and our memories of it affect our frame of reference, the frame or window through which we apprehend life. If our frames of reference are too narrow, misshapen, or cluttered, they can literally block off or distort new people, events, institutions, activities, and ideas. Sometimes, we outgrow a given perception, yet its power continues to affect us. Here are a couple of personal examples.

In the ninth grade, I was the smallest boy in my class. From this, I concluded that it wasn't safe for me to play football—at least not on junior or senior high school teams. Even though I grew ten inches my sophomore year in high school, the early thought stayed with me, which precluded a lucrative career for me in the National Football League. I'm still resentful that no one clarified for me the error of my perception at the time.

To cite a second example, my older brother Bob was bigger, more coordinated, and more attractive than I was. He would sometimes pause in what he was doing, look at me carefully, shudder, and say, "Ooh, you're ugly." He said this seriously and often, and that idea implanted itself in my consciousness. Even though I developed matinee idol good looks later in life, looking in the mirror I still said to myself, "Ooh, you're ugly."

So I hope you get this idea: we are shaped by, and can become encumbered by, prior experiences—so much so that our ability to process information in the present can be affected. It behooves us to understand how our cumulative pasts are affecting our lives in the present moment.

God in His Heaven

The important area that we concentrate on in this book is the matter of a Higher Being and what our stance might or should be in regard to that Being. I hope I've made my point clearly enough by this time that I want you to revisit your thoughts and feelings on this subject and be ready to adjust them—reset your GPS, so to speak. Change your recipe. Adjust that investment portfolio.

Our focus in this book is the God of Abraham, Isaac and Jacob—the God of the Bible. Have you ever wondered why human beings believe in gods generally? Every society, every country, every people back to prehistoric times has believed in a higher power of some kind. I can suggest one answer: perhaps we perceive that life, with all of its complexity and variety, couldn't just happen. Something had to conceive of and activate it. Apparently, every culture, every society has pondered this and similar questions about the origins of things, and assigned responsibility to a god or a set of gods for the creating, managing, and sustaining of life. No other answer must have seemed logical or probable.

Evolutionists, scientists and geneticists, to be fair, sometimes dispute this idea—the idea that, wondrous creatures that we are, we couldn't just happen. They agree that we *have* happened, of course, but in their view, our chemical/biological/genetic profiles have been evolving for millions of years, so of course they're pretty well refined and operational by this time. They should be.

To the ancient Greeks, a family of gods led by Zeus (the Thunderer, God of the Sky) lived on Mount Olympus and governed (and interfered with) the affairs of human beings—sometimes very directly. In the Greek pantheon, members of the family of gods presided over different things: Poseidon, the sea; Ares, war; Athena, wisdom; Artemis, the hunt; Aphrodite, love and beauty; Dionysus, wine; and so on.

Everywhere in the world, on every continent, we find evidence of religion. The evidence is in holy books and artifacts dedicated to religious beliefs, including Christianity, Islam, Hinduism, Buddhism, Judaism, and many others. Great art and architecture celebrate these and other religious systems, individuals, and events. Similar evidence can be found on the walls of caves. Archeologists excavate new findings virtually every day.

A striking, inspirational example of art created to celebrate God is the ceiling of the Sistine Chapel, commissioned by Pope Julius II and painted by Michelangelo between 1508 and 1512. Whatever the pope's motivation in commissioning the project, what matters is the simple fact that the painting came to be at all and that it is so masterfully executed—all five thousand square feet of it! What matters too is what the painting expresses: depictions of momentous events in scripture from Creation, through the Flood, to the coming of Christ, all of them attesting to the faith of the one who painted them. Michelangelo was *inspired* in the conception and execution of the scenes he created.

Cathedrals, pyramids, Mayan temples, Stonehenge, the mysterious *moai* statues on Easter Island, the giant statue of Buddha in Leshan, China—all were created by human beings to give physical shape to extra-human power and authority. Other records and artifacts of religious thought and belief: histories, literature, architecture, music, sculpture—all testify to our apparent need to conceive of or discover--and often worship—spiritual forces.

Experiences of God and Religion

So humankind's collective experience has reflected belief in God (or gods) and has found expression in countless ways. The beauty, variety, and volume of this expression attest to its importance in bringing meaning to people's lives.

The task ahead of us now is to look at that "something" through the lens of our own experience and see what conclusions we can draw. Clearly, artists, kings and queens, conquerors and conquered, priests and subjects have been shaped by their involvement with their gods and God.

Here is an example of such involvement. I have seen a generation of young people raised in our church. My wife, Marsha, was our director of children's ministries for a time, and she now sees students graduating high school whose diapers she changed in the nursery years ago. We see the influence of the church on the character and outlook of these young people. Does that influence vary, both in kind and intensity? Of course it does, but in all cases, the church experience appears to affect those exposed to it.

In our Sunday school class nearly twenty years ago, one of our members was pregnant with a baby she and her husband named Nathan. Today in our service, we blessed Nathan as a young man who is about to go on a mission trip to Greece—to assist those living in a large refugee camp there. I won't share with you the thoughts *I* was having when I was Nathan's age, but I can assure you they had nothing to do with assisting refugees far from my home, far from my extensive and well-padded comfort zone.

I understand that the religious impulse can evolve as a "nature or nurture" consideration. That is, some people by their unique natures develop along paths few would predict, and others can be seen as products of a specific kind of what I'm calling "nurturance." My daughter Annie illustrates this idea. She is loving, clear-headed, money-saving, driven, and accomplished (Latin scholar and teacher). Where did such qualities and tendencies come from? I can't say definitively, but I believe that the "nurture" part of the equation—whether it occurs in a church or not—matters. Like Nathan's, Annie's life in the faith mattered, and continues to matter. It appears that a given soul, much like a plant, needs both its genetic "instructions" (nature) as well as careful attention (nurture) if it is to achieve its full potential.

Hopefully, the Twain Shall Meet

Daniel Taylor has written a book called *The Myth of Certainty: The Reflective Christian & the Risk of Commitment.*[6] Taylor describes two subcultures in modern life: conservative Christians and secularists (the latter are those who do not acknowledge or subscribe to a religious component in life). The former subculture is often characterized by faith and belief, the other by a "just the facts" approach, symbolized by the disciplines of science and mathematics.

According to Taylor, each of these subcultures has established an orthodoxy. An orthodoxy is an accepted theory, doctrine, or practice, subscribed to and lived out by individuals in each respective subculture. In their ways, these orthodoxies can comprise barriers to communication and potential common ground between them. It's possible that your experience with God and the church has been colored by exposure to one of these camps or the other, and that your resulting orthodoxy reflects that particular color.

Often the two subcultures collide when young people leave home for higher education. Young people can be part of a church in their formative years and then go off to work or higher education and find themselves in another "marketplace of ideas," exposed to what can be radically different schools of thought, expressed by articulate members of the other subculture Taylor describes, the secular humanists.

Those who acquire or maintain religious orientations need not be daunted by this. Religious people, contrary to the opinions of some, don't check their brains at any door as they go through life. (Thomas Jefferson is thought to have said to his nephew, "Question with boldness even the existence of a god; because, if there be one, he must more approve the homage of reason, than that of blindfolded fear.") To be a believer is to hold oneself to the same standards of logic, reason, and resulting commitment as secular people. We will return to this idea in a later chapter.

Early Church Life, Revisited

Church can be both a starting and ending place for forming our ultimate ideas about God. Perhaps especially in modern culture, church is not always the most welcoming of places. We listen to a sermon or message, and sometimes the sermon communicates less-than-positive information about ourselves, mainly that we're bad (sinners) and in need of something called salvation. Some can find this bothersome, thinking, "Am I really this bad?"

Regardless of how we answer that question (about our relative goodness or badness) we've seen that a couple of millennia ago, God came to earth in the form of Jesus of Nazareth and suffered the punishment for humankind's bad behavior. In acknowledging this, and agreeing to follow God's commands, we are granted salvation and eternal life in heaven. This is why Jesus is called The Redeemer. He takes our individual histories, checkered as they are, and redeems them with his own innocent blood.

Christianity and other religions can look and sound like pretty exclusive clubs. Initially, at least, we may wonder why they would want us as members (there's an old joke whose punchline is, "I wouldn't belong to any club that would have me as a member"). In many churches, people are usually pretty well-dressed and appear to have their lives in good order. It can be forbidding for those of us who may not yet have all our ducks arranged in such neat rows. By contrast, I like the idea that Christianity is or should be "One beggar telling another where to find bread."

Jesus of Nazareth certainly focused his attention not on the "haves" of his world, but on the "have nots." As you'll see later, He welcomed and ate with prostitutes, tax collectors, and sinners, explaining that healthy people didn't need a physician, that He had come to claim the lost and the suffering.

To mention another possible, early impression of yours, scripture teaches that judgment does await us all, both churched and unchurched. In church we may hear that we will be judged favorably or unfavorably, and if we have the misfortune to be included in the second group, there's the hellish business about lakes of fire, demons, pitchforks, and such like. Hell fire and damnation. If given a choice between hearing about that in church or watching the Ravens play the Steelers, we're probably going to opt for the game.

Those who, from an early age, have had such things as the threat of judgment and hell hanging over them, may not be in the most favorable position to take another view of God, church, and religion. As I just said, if we've been told to stay on the straight and narrow path or we'll burn in hell forever—well, no thank you. We'll take that curvier path.

It's also possible that you've never been to church and never heard of or thought about God or Jesus at all—so you have no negative experiences to overcome. If this is true of you, you too may have come to the right place!

Objectivity

Regardless of how your frame of reference has formed to this point, I'll continue to ask you to look at God and spirituality with new eyes. As much as you can, look past what may be negative earlier experiences and perceptions, and consider again. Try to be objective. Being objective means considering something without coloring it with prior thoughts and feelings. It means coming to conclusions based on a fresh look.

Most of us resist the Eeyore syndrome. We like to think that we carry minimal baggage—of whatever size, weight, and content. We prefer to see ourselves as positive, clear-eyed observers of life as it is. The reality *you* see, however, is not the reality that *I* see. Your eyes are better than mine, for example. I can't see much of anything without these glasses. The same can be said of hearing; you have the hearing of an eagle, and I'm basically deaf as a stone.

And of course I don't mean just physical seeing and hearing. I mean *interpreting* what is seen and heard in what can be a prejudicial manner. This is what we really need to be watchful of, all of us. We see differently because of everything we've lived through. You can enjoy banana cream pie, for example, because you've never been hit in the face with one, as I have.

Pies in the face notwithstanding, we can try to be objective. To look at God or any other subject in as non-prejudicial a manner as possible, we need to be as clear-eyed and in the moment as we can be. We need to stand as clear of preconceptions and prejudices—baggage—as we can. That "pre" prefix is important, remember: it means that we are conceiving of and judging before all the evidence is in.

There is no such thing as pure objectivity. What that word means is that we can look at matters in a non-emotional, dispassionate manner. We are never going to arrive at a purely objective, unemotional, Mr. Spockian kind of objectivity. We can, however, review our memory banks, with their attendant emotional components. We can do regular study, sifting and re-evaluating, making sure our maps of the territory still match the reality. We can try to de-weaponize banana cream pie.

The Problem of the Present Moment

As we saw in Chapter 1, many of us are preoccupied most of the time. We have these texts and emails to respond to. At any given moment, our mental and emotional processing centers are whirring away, playing old tapes, responding to new ones, having attendant feelings, as well as going about the business of classifying and sorting new information. We perceive through that maelstrom of activity. It is little wonder that the pictures we see can be fuzzy and that our subsequent thoughts, actions, and decisions are formed in part on the basis of old, possibly inaccurate information.

Let me say that again:

> We perceive through that maelstrom of activity. It is little wonder that the pictures we see can be fuzzy and that our subsequent thoughts, actions, and decisions are formed in part on the basis of old, possibly inaccurate information.

And remember the sheer data overload that we experience in the digital age. Maybe my point about being able to stop and think is simply wrong-headed, but to me, it looks like we choose to drink from the firehose of information coming to us every day online, through social media, and from other sources. We appear to have little appetite for considering information carefully. There's too much of it, yet many remain addicted to it. We are habituated to it; we may not be aware of how habitual (perhaps unthinking) our reliance on it has become.

David Allen's book *Getting Things Done* addresses another facet of this issue.[7] In Allen's view, anything we perceive that requires attention or fixing (such as the clutter in my garage) becomes an open loop in our consciousness until we manage to resolve it. A tweet is an open loop until we respond to it. Once I tweet in response, or actually do something to reduce the clutter in the garage, the open loop closes, and I have one less thing on my mind, one less item of baggage to weigh me down.

We can't respond effectually to every social media message that comes to us. Let me say this again: *we can't respond effectually to every social media message that comes to us.*

Rather than being weighed down and overloaded (by posts and tweets and emails) we need to be mentally and emotionally agile. In an attempt to respond and resolve something, of necessity we often have to do lightning-fast identifying, labeling, and classifying: "Oh, she's a Republican," or "Of course he feels that way—he's a Yankee fan," or "That's a pit bull—don't go near him." Of necessity, we create linguistic and intellectual storage bins to hold our ideas, but often too rigidly and with too little opacity (i.e., the walls are hard to see through).

A term for this sorting activity is "compartmentalizing," although it has the additional connotation of separating ideas and not being able to see that one contradicts another. For example, we can say on one hand, "No human being ever has the right to jeopardize the life of another," and in the next breath say, "We need to optimize the bombing of selected, high-value Taliban targets in Afghanistan."

How these sorting bins get built, decorated, and enlarged (or diminished) depends on processing capacity (i.e., our ability to think and the time needed to do so), related events, relationships we have (both positive and negative), and our unique personalities. Often, all further thought about a topic can effectively cease once it's labeled and boxed.

In recent times, the concept of a meme has emerged. My understanding is that a meme is another word for the sorting bins we just discussed: it's an idea (verbal or pictorial or musical) that ostensibly communicates a commonly agreed-upon truth: the smartphone addict, the harried multitasker, the woman who has it all (husband, family, career). These are relatively modern memes. They comprise communication shorthand, a medium that we should be careful with in the interest of real objectivity.

Watch Your Language

You recall our lucid, informative discussion about words and referents from earlier in this chapter. Language is an important processing tool at our disposal for determining meaning and maintaining a highly functional frame of reference. Most of us have watched toddlers develop language. We've seen their delight at being able to build and enlarge their boxes of ideas. Learning that things have names brings order and control heretofore unknown to them. Remember Helen Keller learning that "water" meant the cool liquid splashing into her hands, as Annie Sullivan kept signing "W A T E R" into them.

You'll recall that a referent is the real thing to which a word refers. Helen Keller got the crucial connection between the signing Annie was doing, connecting it to the sensation of water gushing over her hands. Think how life expanded for Helen in that moment! She could learn the names of the people and things in her world and develop the sense of control that comes from that learning.

Remember what I said before about those who use a term and can't identify its referent. That's right: they don't know what they're talking about! This doesn't stop many people. I like this quotation, often attributed to either Abraham Lincoln or Mark Twain: "Better to remain silent and be thought a fool than to speak and remove all doubt."

Words have both denotative and connotative meanings. Denotative meanings are the definitions in the dictionary. Connotative meanings are what a given word suggests. Here are some words whose denotative meanings are pretty similar:

slim
slender
svelte
thin
skinny
emaciated
bony
skeletal

All of these words refer to the quality of not weighing very much. But do you see the difference in their suggestions? Would you prefer to be called "slender" or "skeletal"?

Language is also figurative. This means that writers and speakers use terms that are not literally true to create a given effect. Of a person who appears to lack courage, they may say "She doesn't have any guts!" In reality, the individual in question probably has a spleen, lungs, heart, and a thyroid gland. But "guts" has the greater emotional charge.

So in our attempts to revisit, study, and re-evaluate our potential prejudices and beliefs, we need to watch both our language and the language of others.

To review, our subject in this book is the decision we may come to make about God. In life, we hear arguments, testimonies, and histories that bear on this decision. As we encounter them, we need to be prepared to evaluate them, in part with the tools we've just been considering. Is it clear what a given speaker or writer is referring to? Does he or she offer examples? Is the language clear and concise, or does it make an emotional appeal through words clearly chosen for their connotative weight? Is a meme used that everyone allegedly understands?

In speaking of God, Jesus, Christianity, religion, spirituality—we need to demand of those who speak to us that they say what they mean. To use the grammar school phrase, we'll ask them to "concretize their abstractions."

Prejudice

Sometimes, we approach situations with fear and mistrust because we lack information. My only information about Republicans when I was growing up came from my father, who was a dyed-in-the-wool Roosevelt Democrat. He didn't think highly of President Eisenhower; the fact that Ike was a Republican was all my dad needed. No more thinking needed; that's who and what Ike was to him. No open mind there. That box was clearly labeled and sealed. No air in the form of a differing opinion could penetrate it.

I spent a good bit of time in the Deep South as a human resources manager. Sometimes in hearing descriptions of questionable conduct, an individual would identify a given person with the phrase "black guy." To the speaker, that was all the explanation I required as to the potential guilt of the person under discussion. Nothing more to say. Labeled, locked down, and sealed. Air-tight.

If you have God, Christianity, church, and religion locked down and labeled, I'll ask you to unpack some prior conceptions and be willing to formulate some new ones.

Let's look at a couple of other dimensions of our frames of reference—positions we hold, roles we're cast into—and be clear about how all they affect the decision-making process. Again, this is in the service of making sure a given mental map is accurately representing its territory.

In my business and professional life, I've been to hundreds of staff meetings. In a staff meeting, the heads of various departments meet and discuss current happenings in their own departments and hear about needs and issues in other departments—all, of course, for the good of the organization as a whole. I've attended staff meetings that included heads of human resources, operations, finance, safety, and maintenance departments.

The department heads in attendance perceive the meeting through the lens of their own set of needs. Operations thinks that Safety is strangling them with rules that are too rigid. Finance worries that HR is throwing money out the window on programs designed to improve employee relations. Operations thinks that Maintenance is slowing production; they just can't understand why they have to lubricate and repair those machines.

Staff meetings bring together arguably the best minds in the organization, but these minds are often open only to the ideas that will further their own agendas. The frame of reference that should prevail is the good of the organization as a whole. But often attendees are too busy holding their hands too close to their respective vests, protecting their own territories.

Typecasting

In our working lives, we are HR managers, operations managers, safety managers, and so on, and through these limited frames of reference, we filter our lives in our organizations accordingly. In the movie *The Breakfast Club,* we see other sets of filters in operation.

In the film, we find an assortment of high school students spending Saturday together in detention. They provide a spectrum of types: we come to know the jock, the delinquent, the prom queen, the nerd—and one who defies easy classification (I refer to the Ally Sheedy character, who comes to detention because she has nowhere else to go!).

Just like the department heads in the staff meeting, each brings his or her own agenda to the day in detention. Just like business or political affiliations, the types they are assigned limit their ability to interact positively with others.

The actor Anthony Michael Hall plays the scholarly nerd, and Molly Ringwald plays the prom queen. At one point, the group is discussing who each is, explaining why they find it difficult to occupy the roles that they are apparently assigned in the high school culture. The prom queen discusses how hard it is to meet the standards of her high-society friends, saying that the nerd and the others can't relate to the pressure she feels.

Hall's character listens for a time in disbelief and then says, "You're so conceited, Claire; you're so full of yourself!" To him, she has allowed herself to become almost another species, basically blind to the other creatures around her. In the fullness of herself, she finds it difficult or impossible to consider the perspectives of others.

Indeed, the students in the breakfast club are full of the roles they play, that they've assigned to themselves, or that they've been consigned to by others: parents, peer groups, teachers. If there is open-mindedness and objectivity in them to understand the needs and perceptions of others, in the beginning, it's hard to see. The movie is the story of how that widening of perception occurs.

We've all known people who are full of different things. When we think of ourselves, we can recall being full of anger, of hatred, of praise, of resentment, of love, of information. And just like the characters in the movie, we have been full of a given character or persona. If the character you've become has grown too rigid and locked into a given persona (such as one of the people in *The Breakfast Club*), begin to think of how you might break out, how you might, as Jesus recommended, develop new eyes to see and ears to hear.

Summary

Our degree of open-mindedness can be affected by affiliations of various kinds: with one school or another, one political party or another, one of Daniel Taylor's subcultures, the sacred or the secular. Open-mindedness can be affected by our affiliation with cultural and ethnic groups. They are affected by the roles we cast ourselves into or are cast into by others. They are affected by our stages of emotional and intellectual development.

As we begin our study of God and spirituality, try to become more aware of your frame of reference: how you're perceiving the people, events, and ideas of your life. Soon we will hear Jesus say, "I am the way, the truth, and the life." As we wait, we can try to be clear about the ways, truths, and lives we've lived to this point.

Chapter Three

God in Spirit and in Truth

God is spirit, and his worshippers must worship
in the Spirit and in truth. (John 4:24)
I am the way and the truth and the life. No one comes
to the Father except through me. (John 14:6)
Father, into your hands I commit my spirit. (Luke 23:46)

Jack

Marsha and I had Jack, our Labrador, for more than eleven years. He was not a purebred Lab—his mother was, but unfortunately, Jack's father was never identified. Given the size that Jack grew to (quite large), we suspect that his father may have been a Rottweiler.

We all loved Jack; it's hard to resist telling a bunch of Jack stories here, but I will.

He's been gone now for some nine years. He developed a large tumor on his heart, which spread and did him in. He was cremated, and his ashes are in a carved wooden box on my bookshelf behind me.

Once we knew that our veterinarians could do nothing more for him, we had Jack put down, as the saying goes. At the veterinarian's office, the staff left me and Jack alone in a starkly lit room, with a metal table in the middle. When they were ready to proceed, I had them lay Jack on his side on the table so he could see me. I wanted to be looking into his eyes when he died.

I was. His kind brown eyes were looking steadily into mine as the shot was administered, and I watched the light behind his eyes dim and then go out.

Frame of Reference

In Chapter 1, we talked about the nature of decisions. We concluded that it's possible to make and commit to them. We said that there are some things that are too important not to decide, and that a conscious decision about God might be one of those. We talked about how we invest ourselves in different ways and said that it's often wise to make sure our portfolios are giving us optimum returns.

In Chapter 2, we talked about objectivity, in part how difficult it is to be objective, especially in our social media-dominated culture. We discussed semantics and language, referring to the advisability of knowing what we're talking about—when we talk to others and when we talk to ourselves. I asked that you think anew about your frame of reference, suggesting that if you hadn't done any modifications to that frame in a while, it might be time to do so, making sure that your maps and territories are still in sync.

Making adjustments to that frame of reference may be easier said than done. It's not unlike rewiring a house, this business of making modifications to your frame of reference, your typical way of thinking. Doing so takes us into the realm of brain chemistry and genetics. Apparently, habitual ways of thinking strengthen in our brains over time, developing their own neural pathways, along which messages travel. Unless a different thought occurs to us, a given impulse or electrical signal is going to follow the same neural pathway it has in the past.

You could decide, for example, to take a different route to work. As you make the required left turns and right turns, speed up or slow down, your brain gets to work drawing a new map. And from that point on, it will follow the new map until you tell it otherwise. It has constructed a new set of neural pathways for the particular task of getting you to work.

Again, in order to handle the extraordinary workload we place on them, our brains have to use paths or roadways they've always used with certain information; they don't have time to create a new one for what they perceive to be familiar information.

So one contributor to our being the people we are is the neural architecture of our individual brains, which facilitates the way we usually think. In addition to this basic architecture, the brain has the ability to create new roadways in response to new directions we provide. In time, that new way of getting to work can become as automatic as the old one.

The Birds and the Beaks

With our unique DNA footprint, however, we basically have to play the hand we've been dealt by our mothers and fathers; that is, our particular concentration of genes, housed in thread-like chromosomes, living in cells, dictates the various human traits that we have (such as eye and hair color). But—cue the orchestra—evolution can also play a role. Genetic content can change over time in response to different stimuli. To create a simple example, a certain species of bird's beak size and shape are products of its heredity: what it got from its parents.

However, if environmental factors dictate that the bird change its feeding habits over a span of time, having to poke its beak into logs in search of insects, for example, then both the size and the shape of the beak may change to facilitate the change demanded by the bird's environment. This is called natural selection, and it's a central tenet of evolutionary theory.

Apparently, the way genetic material is affected by various stimuli over time can be tracked, and often a great deal of time (as in hundreds or thousands of years) must pass before significant alterations in genetic material can be detected among members of a species, along with the resulting physical and mental changes.

Again, when we speak of neural pathways, we talk about the channels or highways upon which messages travel. When we add genetics, we talk about the messaging material itself. Genes carry our individual DNA, the units of heredity that determine our physical, mental, and emotional makeup (again, two of these from our mothers and two from our fathers).

Here is why I include this material about genetics and brain function: It's because our subject in this book is finding God, in places we may not have thought to look before. Now *how* God may be at work in genetic maintenance and adjustment is for others more qualified in this area than I am to determine. But—what if the data on this subject already concludes that we humans do have a genetic predisposition to spirituality? That seems to be the case[8] and, as such, is wholly relevant to our topic.

It seems unlikely that God would design a predisposition into us that has no endpoint, that He would provide a map without a destination. He of course is the Final Destination that He wants each of us to reach.

Even my elementary peek at genetics and cell physiology leaves me astounded by the complexity that exists there. Yet we speak of potential change in *behavior* in the most simplistic of terms. We recall Nancy Reagan's slogan for the drug problem decades ago: "Just say no." It's just not that simple; behavior itself is the tangible last step when we discuss our ability to change; for example, living as an atheist as opposed to living like a Christian.

Before anyone can achieve this "tangible last step"—behavioral change—often a great deal of time must pass. In many cases new learning must occur; and, behind the scenes, so to speak, a lot of internal reconstruction, re-wiring and re-mixing of chemicals must occur as well. For the "new," external person to re-emerge, the internal architecture and plumbing must be firmly in place and functioning.

What each of our respective, individual gene profiles indicate are our predispositions, our tendencies, and our potentials. They are the coded programs that God designed into us, uniting the DNA of our respective parents to bring about the unique individuals that we are. While each of us is genetically unique, apparently environmental factors and behaviors can adjust our genetic profiles to produce altered traits and attendant behaviors. Understand that we are not talking here about a "macro" level change such as an alteration in beak size. What is true in this wider context, however, may be true on the micro level as well, affecting behavioral components such as perception and thinking. Change is possible; we can affect it—apparently on a number of different levels.

God thus appears to be Designer, Builder, and Remodeler; He is the Creator, and we are the creations and often the *re*-creations. Chances are He is not finished with any of us.

No Neural Highway in the Sky

I may be getting ahead of myself. It's possible that your perception of God has been a negligible one, in the sense that you've never felt a need to consider Him at all. Neural pathways may be weedy and over grown, if indeed they exist at all.

In earlier times in our country and elsewhere, this was not the case. Depending on the exact time and place, God apparently traveled much down those pathways. You will recall, for example, that we wrote "One nation, under God," into our Pledge of Allegiance, and that our Declaration of Independence includes the phrase, "We hold these truths to be self-evident, that all men are created equal, that they are endowed by their Creator with certain unalienable Rights, that among these are Life, Liberty and the pursuit of Happiness."

The key terms here are "created" and "their Creator." These words mean that humankind didn't just happen; we humans received a specific "endowment" from our Creator. Occupying, at the time, such a prominent place in our collective national mind, the endowment also included certain expected behaviors. As a populace under God, we were expected to be good. We were supposed to obey, among many other things, the Ten Commandments. Jesus even said to His followers, "Be perfect, therefore, as your Father in heaven is perfect" (Matthew 5:48).

We weren't, of course, perfect. But our forefathers for the most part had the God of Abraham, Isaac, and Jacob on their minds and in their hearts. The Bible was part of the expected education young people were to receive. In 1636, Harvard College was conceived of and developed as an institution to prepare people for the ministry. The Puritans arriving in New England—some seventeen thousand of them by that time—perceived a sure and certain need for more people to preach the Gospel (the good news of Christ's arrival).

Our forefathers seemed to know much more clearly who they were, Whom they belonged to, and how they were to behave.

This is less true today. Religion isn't the guiding force that it was, and we aren't the people we used to be. As individuals, we seem much more scattered—unfocused—than we used to be. I commented earlier on all the things that compete for our attention, including smartphones and our seeming insistence on cultivating presences on Facebook, Instagram, Twitter, QZone, Tumblr, and other social media platforms.

Our national leaders bear little resemblance to their predecessors of long ago. Given the world and time you were born into, if you haven't developed a clear concept of God and His role in our lives, that's to be understood. But know that this wasn't always the case (in our country and elsewhere) and that it need not continue to be the case.

Our forefathers on the new North American continent weren't perfect in their worship practices. We could quarrel, for example, with their practice of burning people at the stake, people perceived as heretics and witches. But many of them at least had the ability to pay attention (our forefathers, not necessarily those convicted of heresy and sorcery), to ask the serious questions as to who they should be, Whom they should serve, how they should live, and ultimately what their lives should mean.

You may have heard the word *predilection*. A predilection is a tendency toward something, a disposition, if you will. To return to our genetics/heredity topic, it does appear that prolonged experience of a certain kind and intensity can actually direct genetic change. The experience of lengthy periods of meditation, for example, may lead not only to increased skill in that concrete practice (both its behavioral and intellectual content), but also to corresponding adjustments affecting heredity—to changes in our DNA. This is interesting in light of Jesus's suggestion, "Be perfect, even as your Father in heaven is perfect." Perhaps perfect becomes as perfect does.

Should you wish to learn more about genetics and its application to belief and spirituality, it is explored more deeply in *The God Gene*, written by Dean Hamer in 2004.[9]

God in Spirit and in Truth

Jesus says this in the Gospel of John: "God is spirit, and his worshippers must worship in the Spirit and in truth" (John 4:24). In Merriam-Webster, we read that the definition of *spirit* is "an animating or vital principle held to give life to physical organisms." What I saw when Jack died was the "animating or vital principle" leave his body. His spirit was a fact; it was there (in him), and then it was gone. I don't think it disappeared. Rather, I think it left him and went elsewhere.

Early in the book of Genesis, we read what God did after creating the earth and everything in it: "Then the Lord God formed a man from the dust of the ground and breathed into his nostrils the breath of life, and the man became a living being" (Genesis 2:7). Thus the biblical view is that man from his beginning was "inspired" by God.

Earlier we mentioned that, in the Gospel of John, Jesus is trying to explain to Nicodemus (a Pharisee, an elder in the Jewish religious hierarchy) about new birth in the faith, about the need for people to be "born again" to take their places in the Kingdom of God: "Very truly I tell you, no one can enter the kingdom of God unless they are born of water and the Spirit. Flesh gives birth to flesh, but the Spirit gives birth to spirit" (John 3:5–7).

And then this interesting addition: "The wind blows wherever it pleases. You hear its sound, but you cannot tell where it comes from or where it is going. So it is with everyone born of the Spirit" (John 3:8). Remember from a moment ago that God "inspired" the first man—literally breathed life into him. In His comments about the wind, Jesus may be saying that looking for God in tangible, physical form may not always be fruitful. If it were, perhaps Jesus would not have been given His mission.

As we said in Chapter 1, God expressed Himself most fully in Jesus. For His redemptive purposes, God in Jesus entered our world as a helpless baby, born to a poor couple in Palestine, in a stable, no less. And understand that Jesus is historical fact, not fiction. His life and ministry are recorded in the Gospels of Matthew, Mark, Luke, and John, and He is referred to by other historians of His time (e.g., Tacitus and Josephus). A place you can access this information concisely is *The Case for Christ,* written by Lee Strobel in 1998.

Just the Facts?

Strobel was a longtime investigative reporter in Chicago and also a longtime atheist and skeptic. In *The Case for Christ,* he applies his background in investigative reporting to Jesus and Christianity. His method is to search out and interview acknowledged scholars who have devoted much of their professional careers to exploring different aspects of Jesus's life. Strobel's analysis includes the eyewitness record, the documentary evidence, the corroborating evidence, scientific evidence—and even the rebuttal evidence for Jesus's life and ministry. His work can be summarized as "Here's the evidence; you decide."

Jesus, God, and the Holy Spirit are One. If Jesus is fact, then God and the Holy Spirit must be as well. If you have trouble grasping this idea, you aren't alone.

As Father, Son, and Spirit, God is referred to as a "triune" God: this means three in one, or God the Father, Son, and Holy Spirit. C. S. Lewis says that this triune nature is "not a static thing—not even a person—but a dynamic, pulsating activity, a life, almost a kind of drama."

Here is how Lewis describes the Holy Spirit and His role in the trinity:

> This third Person is called, in technical language, the Holy Ghost or the "spirit" of God. Do not be worried

> or surprised if you find it (or Him) rather vaguer or more shadowy in your mind than the other two.... In the Christian life you are not usually looking at Him: He is always acting through you. If you think of the Father as something "out there," in front of you, and of the Son as someone standing at your side, helping you to pray, trying to turn you into another son, then you have to think of the third Person as something inside you, or behind you.[10]

In the first letter of John in the Bible's New Testament, John tells us, "Whoever does not love does not know God, because God is love" (1 John 4:8). In other words, God is not simply Spirit, but Spirit of a definite kind and with a definite purpose. In this regard, C. S. Lewis says, "God is love, and that love works through men—especially through the whole community of Christians. But this spirit of love is, from all eternity, a love going on between the Father and the Son."[11]

Jesus says that He (God in human form) is "the way, the truth, and the life." He is, in other words, the method, the reality, and the life force itself. As in my example of Jack, perhaps we see this most clearly through its absence. Life has always been, it seems, difficult; we need a method to live it as we were designed to. We need the truth of it, not synthetic, unreliable substitutes; we need inspiration, the very breath of life. As He himself says it, Jesus *is* this truth, this way, this life.

God is revealed perhaps most clearly and thoroughly in the Bible. To provide baseline information that you may not have had before, I'm going to offer now a shortened summary of it.

The Five Books of Moses

In the Bible, God creates the heavens and the earth. Then He creates man and strives to be in continuous, harmonious relationship with him. This relationship is depicted in a variety of ways in the Bible, which is really many books in one. It is a library of volumes, each of which tells of a different aspect of this ongoing relationship between

God and man, and which tells of those aspects in different voices and different forms such as narratives, psalms (songs), proverbs, and letters.

You've noticed that after quoting something from the Bible, I include a name (for which book of the Bible I'm referring to—e.g., Matthew or John), and then two numbers separated by a colon (:). Should you want to learn more about a particular topic, these numbers enable you to go to the appropriate book in the Bible and find the specific chapter and verse.

The first five books of the Bible are sometimes called the Pentateuch or the Five Books of Moses, and consist of Genesis, Exodus, Leviticus, Numbers, and Deuteronomy. Tradition holds that these five books were written by Moses.

Genesis is the "In the beginning" book. This is where you'll find the garden of Eden story, about how God envisioned the garden to be the permanent dwelling place for Adam, Eve, and their descendants. That didn't work out. The concept of Original Sin comes from Genesis, referring to the fact that Adam and Eve sinned in the garden by eating the forbidden fruit from the Tree of the Knowledge of Good and Evil. They are seduced into doing so by the devil, or Satan. In the garden, Satan appears as a serpent, tricking Eve into eating of the forbidden fruit.

Murder rears its ugly head in Genesis, as Cain, child of Adam and Eve, murders his brother Abel out of jealousy (God apparently favored Abel's sacrifice to Cain's). In subsequent generations, we meet Jacob, father of the Twelve Tribes of Israel, led by Jacob's twelve sons. The Holy Land is divided into twelve sections, named after each of these twelve sons.

The youngest son, Joseph, is he who wears the Amazing Technicolor Dream Coat. Joseph's brothers, unkindly enough, try to kill him by throwing him down a well—like Cain, they too were jealous: of that Technicolor Dream Coat and other signs of Jacob's love for their brother. Bad luck for them: Joseph is rescued and becomes second in command to Egypt's Pharaoh. All the brothers are later reconciled.

Exodus tells of the enslavement of the Hebrew people in Egypt and of Moses, who was born Jewish but raised as Egyptian royalty and eventually chosen by God to be the prophet who leads the Israelites out of Egypt. Moses demanded that Pharaoh release his people, but Pharaoh refused, which resulted in Moses and his brother Aaron bringing ten horrible plagues down on Egypt, the last of which resulted in the death of Pharaoh's son. Pharaoh finally acceded to Moses's demand ("let my people go") but then changed his mind and sent his army in pursuit of them.

You may have heard about how God parted the waters of the Red Sea, allowed the Jewish nation to pass through on dry land, then drowned the Egyptian army that was pursuing them.

This had to be harrowing for the fleeing Israelites, even though they made it to safety. But thereafter, things didn't work out wonderfully well for them. They wandered in the desert, some thinking that they'd have been better off in their enslaved condition, even turning aside from their faith. At one point, they created a golden calf to worship instead of the one true God. Moses discovered this event (the creating and worshipping of the golden calf) after coming down from Mount Sinai with the Ten Commandments. He wasn't pleased.

The book of Leviticus lacks the drama of Exodus. No Red Seas parting; no plagues; no hurling of the Ten Commandments, written as those were on tablets of stone. Leviticus, by contrast, is like a legal tract. In chapter 7, Moses finds it necessary to spell out in exacting detail the offerings brought by tribal leaders to the newly finished tabernacle.

When I say "exacting detail," I mean it. Speaking of preparing a bull for offering, we read in Chapter 8 of Leviticus, "Then Moses slaughtered the ram and splashed the blood against the sides of the altar. He cut the ram into pieces and burned the head, the pieces and the fat. He washed the internal organs and the legs with water and burned the whole ram on the altar. It was a burnt offering, a pleasing aroma, a food offering presented to the Lord, as the Lord commanded Moses" (Leviticus 8:19–21).

Since God, understandably, was not pleased with how quickly His people turned away in the desert, He thought He had to spell out the law in a very detailed way. So He did, as you just saw. What His people should eat, how they should eat it, how they should worship, where they should worship. Very exacting, very detailed.

Reading Numbers, the fourth book of the Pentateuch, we understand at least partially why the Israelites behaved as they did. The Sinai is not Palm Springs. The Israelites wandered in the forbidding desert for forty years, and most of them died there, menaced by snakes, hostile tribes, the heat, and not least of all, uncertainty about where they were headed and what was to become of them.

One commentator says that the Israelites finally "unraveled" in the desert, going from murmurings about how good things were in Egypt, to open rebellion against Moses and Aaron. Later commentators were to remind their audiences of what happened in the Sinai to the Israelites, using that as a warning to not let it happen again, to obey God's law as it was given and not go their own way.

Some finally do make it to the Promised Land, the land of Canaan, west across the Jordan River, the land which was to be "flowing with milk and honey." The fifth book of the Pentateuch, Deuteronomy, covers this period. Deuteronomy is Moses's summing up. The trials the Israelites had absorbed to that point had to weigh heavily on them, so Moses appears to say, "Okay, you didn't get it the first time; listen carefully this time." And he goes through everything again.

Moses never made it, never crossed over the Jordan. He bequeathed leadership to Joshua, who led the people successfully across the Jordan and to the lives they'd been promised on the other side.

The Covenant

God established his covenant with the Israelites. They were the chosen people. He would be their God, and they would be His people. They were given the Ten Commandments (these are the ones Moses threw at the Israelites after returning from God on Mount Sinai):

1. You shall have no other gods before Me.
2. You shall not make idols.
3. You shall not take the name of the LORD your God in vain.
4. Remember the Sabbath day, to keep it holy.
5. Honor your father and your mother.

6. You shall not murder.
7. You shall not commit adultery.
8. You shall not steal.
9. You shall not bear false witness against your neighbor.
10. You shall not covet.

The Jews wove the commandments and what could be called sub-commandments into every area of life: how to pray, when to pray, how to eat, what to eat, and so on. Jewish religious practices were codified into "the law," and the law was administered by varying levels of religious leaders such as the Pharisees, the scribes, and the Sadducees. There were also councils with varying levels of authority; it was one of these that determined that Jesus would die by crucifixion. The Romans to a large degree let the Jewish leaders administer their own law; in its way, this made governing the often quarrelsome population easier to manage.

Again, the Pentateuch is the first five books of the Old Testament. There are thirty-three more books in the Old Testament. There are twelve so-called history books immediately following the Pentateuch, and in them, we are introduced to major figures such as Saul, Samuel, David, and Solomon, as well as many dimmer lights, kings who ruled what became the two parts of the divided kingdom, Israel and Judah.

Rulers

You recall David, he of David and Goliath fame. In the Old Testament, we see God sometimes appear to fixate on a given individual, sustaining him through any number of grievous situations. David is Exhibit A of this. Defeating Goliath when David was still a boy was necessary and heroic, and we find ourselves wishing that he could have carried over his courage and wisdom to the governance of the nation.

And in some ways, he did. But he also committed adultery with Bathsheba, the wife of one of his military commanders (the child born of this encounter died in infancy). The commander, Uriah, was the staunchest of soldiers. He was summoned to the palace while a battle was in progress. David's thought was that Uriah would sleep with Bathsheba, then naturally assume that any child born afterward would be his. But Uriah insisted on sleeping outside, to honor the sacrifices his soldiers were undergoing while he was away. David came up with an evil Plan B. When Uriah returned to the battle, David instructed his generals to make sure Uriah was placed where the fighting was fiercest—and Uriah consequently dies in battle.

David is later forced to acknowledge his crime. The prophet Nathan confronts him, and David undergoes a period of penance, but he stays in power. We ask ourselves how God could countenance sins like David's; we assume that the perspective He has in these situations is more informed and appropriate than ours.

David was a writer and a musician. We give him credit for many of the Psalms, which comprise a major segment of the Old Testament. Some of us have committed to memory the 23rd Psalm, which is a concise summary of David's walk with God:

> The Lord is my shepherd, I lack nothing.
>
> He makes me lie down in green pastures, he leads me beside quiet waters,
>
> He refreshes my soul. He guides me along the right paths for his name's sake.
>
> Even though I walk through the darkest valley, I will fear no evil, for you are with me; your rod and your staff they comfort me.
>
> You prepare a table before me in the presence of my enemies. You anoint my head with oil; my cup overflows.
>
> Surely your goodness and love will follow me all the days of my life, and I will dwell in the house of the Lord forever.

Throughout much of his life, David found favor with God. With many of the pivotal figures in scripture, we find greatness and incredible weakness coexisting, often in equal measure. David was a great warrior; he was a musician; he was a writer (read the Psalm above again); and unlike many who were to follow him, he showed that he could learn from his mistakes.

Solomon was the tenth son of King David, born in 1010 BC. He is known for wisdom; we recall the story in which he resolves the dispute between two women who each claim to be the mother of a child, by suggesting that the child be cut in half, with each woman receiving one of the halves. He gives the child to the woman who begs that the child be allowed to live, thus signifying that she is the true mother.

Also attesting to Solomon's wisdom are the Proverbs, wise sayings that provide counsel in how to live effectively, obeying God's laws. We find ourselves wondering, however, if he *read* them after he'd written them. In part to form strategic alliances with other nations, Solomon entered into any number of treaties, cementing them with royal marriages and gifts that included concubines. By some counts, Solomon had seven hundred wives and three hundred concubines.

Solomon also oversaw the building of the First Temple, which survived until it was destroyed by the Babylonians some six hundred years before the birth of Christ. Solomon's temple was dedicated to Yahweh (Jehovah), but later, other gods were also worshipped there, including Baal and Asherah. The First Temple lasted nearly five hundred years, as reported by the historian Josephus and others.

Prophets

To say that the people of Israel led something of a checkered existence throughout the Old Testament is the height of understatement. Periodically, God would raise up prophets to try to yank them back to the path He envisioned for them. You perhaps have heard the names Isaiah, Jeremiah, Ezekiel, Daniel, Jonah, Zachariah, and Malachi.

Each of these, not to mention others who do not have dedicated books in the Bible, are deserving of attention and study. Some religious leaders in the New Testament thought that major figures in Jesus's time were Old Testament prophets returning, asking John the Baptist, for example, if he were the prophet Elijah, returning from the dead. He was not; he had his own story to tell, which we will see shortly.

The New Testament

With the coming of Jesus, the law was replaced by the new covenant in Christ. Under this covenant, those who believe need only have faith in Jesus as the Son of God and obey His commandments to retain favor in God's eyes. Both the Jewish and the Roman "establishments" were to see this idea in radically different ways.

Jesus's family tree stretches back to the twelve tribes of Israel, which were led by the twelve sons of Jacob. Jacob was the twin of Esau and the son of Isaac and Rachel. Isaac was the son of "Father Abraham." As we have just seen, the Old Testament includes the stories of great and not-so-great kings (e.g., Saul, David, Solomon); the prophets (Elijah, Jeremiah, et al.); the Psalms; and the Proverbs.

It was important in the emerging church—reflected especially in the Gospel of Matthew—to establish Jesus's lineage in the family of Abraham. So that the Jews would recognize Jesus as the Messiah promised in the Old Testament, Matthew actually lists who "begat" whom, all the way back to "Father Abraham," through Jesse, who was the father of King David, down to another Jacob (the son of Matthan), who "begat" Joseph, Jesus's earthly father.

The New Testament includes the four Gospel stories, written by Matthew, Mark, Luke, and John. These men were either disciples of Jesus or companions of people who were. Matthew, for example, was a tax collector and one of Jesus's original twelve disciples. Mark was a companion and interpreter of Peter, the disciple and the "Rock" upon whom Jesus said He would build His church. As just mentioned, Luke was a physician and a contemporary of the apostle Paul (he who announced himself "crucified with Christ").

The first three Gospels, Matthew, Mark, and Luke, are called the Synoptic Gospels, which means that all three are fairly strict narratives (synopses) that consider Jesus's story as a whole. While I use the word "narrative" to describe them, the Gospels are unique. They are clearly biographical in nature and novel-like in their inclusion of plot and dialogue—but they somehow transcend these genres; each is considerably more than the sum of its respective parts (i.e., character, description, diction, setting, events, recorded facts).

Further, the synoptic Gospels, while they share some source material (the same events often appear in each of them), are quite different in their purposes. Matthew takes pains to establish Jesus's connections to Old Testament prophecies; Mark provides a fast-paced account of Jesus's life, drawing attention to the miracles as testimony to Jesus's divinity; and Luke's Gospel is acknowledged as the most complete historical account of Jesus's life.

The fourth Gospel, written by Jesus's disciple John, brother of James and son of Zebedee, is different in sequence, form, and content, containing much more of Jesus's teaching and preaching. Rather than simply telling Jesus's story, John announces as his stated purpose the establishing of Jesus's divinity, His status as the Son of God. The Gospel of John is the latest of the Gospels, and we envision John having the time to develop perspective, to sum up to his satisfaction both what he had experienced and what he had heard.

Some question why there are four Gospels and not one, since they all tell basically the same story. Skeptics point to the differences in the Gospels as evidence that the Gospel writers couldn't get their stories straight and thus conclude that the stories must be made up.

Other commentators point to the differences as proof of the Gospels' authenticity. One test of the historical accuracy of ancient documents is the level of detail in them, and all the Gospels contain convincing detail, including some that don't paint the most positive of pictures of key figures. This is especially true in the depictions of Jesus's followers, who are often shown in less-than-favorable lights, even though they traveled and ministered with Jesus for more than three years.

The Gospels are followed by the book of Acts, also known as the Acts of the Apostles. Acts describes what happened to Jesus's followers after His Crucifixion and resurrection. It is written by the physician

Luke, the author of the third so-called synoptic Gospel that bears his name. In Acts, we become well-acquainted with the apostle Paul, about whom we'll have much to say later.

The New Testament Letters (the Epistles)

The next section of the New Testament includes the letters of the Apostle Paul, and additional letters (epistles) written by James, Peter, John, and Jude; the book of Hebrews; it concludes with the book of Revelation, which was also written by the disciple John, said to be "the disciple Jesus loved."

The Apostle Paul did something extraordinary. As we saw earlier, he went from being a persecutor of the developing church to its primary spokesperson. He both preached the Gospel and explained it, in letter after letter to believers in the region: two letters to the church in Corinth, two letters to the church in Thessalonica, two letters to his faithful fellow evangelist Timothy. He wrote also to churches in Galatia, Ephesus, Philippi, and Colosse.

The fact that Christianity survived and flourished may not be entirely due to Paul and his ministry, but he exerted a tremendous influence.

In Acts, we read about one of the most remarkable events in the Bible, the coming of the Holy Spirit at Pentecost. Jesus had promised that He would send the Spirit (the Holy Spirit, the Spirit of Truth, the Comforter), to be with the disciples after He returned to the Father. The disciples, who had been less than inspiring prior to this time, simply became new men after the Spirit descended upon them (with "tongues of fire," according to Luke) at Pentecost.

Also in Acts, we first meet Saul of Tarsus. We are introduced to Saul as a young man who was present at and consenting to the martyrdom of Stephen (by stoning). Saul became part of a great persecution at that time of the early church. Luke tells us, "But Saul began to destroy the church. Going from house to house, he dragged off both men and women and put them in prison" (Acts 8:3).

Later in Acts, we meet Saul again on his way to Damascus to

arrest and imprison more followers of Jesus. He was struck blind on the road and heard a voice saying "Saul, Saul, why do you persecute Me?" (Acts 9:3–4).

It is the risen Jesus Who speaks to Saul and tells him in his weakened state to go into Damascus and await further instruction. There he neither eats nor drinks for three days and remains sightless. Jesus calls upon "a certain disciple" named Ananias to go to Saul and baptize him. Ananias is astonished, because he is fully aware of the persecutions wrought by Saul to that point. But Ananias hears Jesus say, "Go! This man is my chosen instrument to proclaim My name to the Gentiles, and their kings, and to the people of Israel. I will show him how much he must suffer for My name" (Acts 9:15–16).

Saul of Tarsus, persecutor of Christians, becomes the apostle Paul, author of much of the New Testament, the very person who was to say the passage I quoted earlier from Galatians: "I am crucified with Christ; it is no longer I who live, but Christ lives in me."

The New Testament concludes with letters from the other writers listed earlier and the book of Revelation. Revelation is written by the disciple John while he was exiled on the island of Patmos. Revelation is the vision given to John of the end times; it describes in graphic detail what will happen at the end of the world.

We've traveled a goodly distance in this chapter. If you were discombobulated by the discussion of genetics and brain function, try not to be. Remember that in this book, we're talking about some possible reordering of your mental maps, a subject of some complexity and importance. As we do, there's no point in pretending that our subject is simple when it's not.

And we've included a rough and incomplete overview of the Bible, complexity on top of complexity! I included the Bible overview, as I remarked earlier, because some readers may not be familiar with its basic outline and content. We will look now at New Testament writings in greater detail.

Chapter Four

Jesus's Life and Times

Jesus loves me, this I know,
for the Bible tells me so.
Little ones to Him belong.
They are weak but He is strong.

Yes, Jesus loves me.
Yes, Jesus loves me.
Yes, Jesus loves me.
The Bible tells me so.
–Anna B. Warner

Jesus Loves *Me*?

The familiar hymn "Jesus Loves Me" existed first as a poem. It was written by Anna B. Warner and appeared first in an 1860 novel (*Say and Seal*) written by Anna's sister, Susan. In the novel, the words are spoken to comfort a dying child. A gentleman named William

Bradbury discovered the poem and added music to it, adding the chorus you see above. The hymn has had countless verses added to it over the decades since it was first written.

I start this chapter with "Jesus Loves Me" because it is the first idea about Jesus that I had. I don't remember asking why He loved me, just that He did.

During my early years in post-WWII America, parents were a bit more casual about child rearing than they are now. My own, for example, didn't pay a lot of attention to what they thought were peripheral issues, things such as personal hygiene, chores, pet care, basic safety, nutrition, orthodontia, curfews—not to mention my first religious instruction.

So I can't imagine that they delivered the song "Jesus Loves Me" to me as part of a formal program of religious instruction. Another part of that instruction was saying grace at mealtime, especially dinner time (because our family tended to be together then). Our prayer was "Dear Lord Jesus, bless this food we eat. Amen."

Sometimes, before we went to bed, my parents would have my brother Bob and I pray, "Now I lay me down to sleep, I pray the Lord my soul to keep. If I should die before I wake, I pray the Lord my soul to take. Amen." I don't remember why we weren't terrified at the prospect of dying in the night, but we weren't.

I must have heard "Jesus Loves Me" in Sunday school or Bible school. It was one of the first references to Jesus that I recall, possibly the very first reference. It may have awakened curiosity as to Who Jesus was.

The Historical Jesus

We did see pictures of Jesus. In fact, one is in my office as we speak. It is one you've probably seen, depicting Jesus praying in the garden. He is kneeling by a large rock, His hands are clasped in front of Him, and He's wearing a purple robe. A beam of light illuminates His head, forming a halo. My parents had this picture in their bedroom for as long as I can remember, and now I have it.

Except Jesus probably didn't look much like the figure in my picture.

Through the years, He's been pictured as one close in appearance, apparently, to those who did the picturing. He was played by the actor Robert Powell in Franco Zeffirelli's 1977 film *Jesus of Nazareth*. Powell was tall and decidedly European in appearance, with piercing blue eyes, pale skin, and long brown hair.

Scholars, archaeologists, and other researchers have hypothesized from a variety of sources what Jesus would have worn (plain, undyed clothing), and that His features would likely have been similar to those of others of His time living in the Eastern Mediterranean. He would not have been pale, given the climate of the region and the amount of time He spent out of doors. He probably did have a beard; some hypothesize that He wouldn't have been large, especially by modern standards. Average height for the time was approximately five foot five or shorter, and weight some 120 pounds.

Appearance aside, Who indeed was He, and is He? Here is Philip Schaff's assessment:

> Jesus of Nazareth, without money and arms, conquered more millions than Alexander the Great, Caesar, Mohammed, and Napoleon; without science and learning, he shed more light on things human and divine than all philosophers and scholars combined; without the eloquence of school, he spoke such words of life as were never spoken before or since, and produced effects which lie beyond the reach of orator or poet; without writing a single line, he set more pens in motion, and furnished themes for more sermons, orations, discussions, learned volumes, works of art, and songs of praise than the whole army of great men of ancient and modern times.[12]

Please read this passage again. I'll wait.

Words are inadequate to express how important Jesus was, and is, during and after His life on earth. Some basic facts are that He was the son of Joseph and Mary. He was raised in the small village of Nazareth, which was a dozen miles or so from the Sea of Galilee. He learned the trade of His father (His earthly father) Joseph, which was carpentry. Some consider this description too narrow, that Joseph was a builder, and that as such he would have worked with metals and stone as well as wood.

Later in life, Jesus referred often to God, His heavenly father, in loving terms. Some credit Jesus's earthly father, Joseph, as being an important model for Jesus of what a father should be.

With several exceptions, nothing in Jesus's boyhood suggested what He would become, as foretold by the prophet Isaiah: "For to us a child is born, to us a son is given, and the government will be on His shoulders. And he will be called Wonderful Counselor, Mighty God, Everlasting Father, Prince of Peace".

We mark recorded time in terms of events occurring before Jesus's birth, and those occurring after. The former used to be called "BC" (before Christ) and "AD" (Anno Domini, or "In the year of our Lord"). More recently, some prefer "BCE" for "Before the Common Era" and "CE" for "Common Era," but the periods themselves—those before Christ's birth and after it—are the same. Those preferring that the times in question be theologically neutral can say that the "C" refers to "Common"; we Christians can say that it refers to "Christ."

These demarcations in time provide an indication of Jesus's influence. One writer, Andrew McLaren, says, "We believe that the history of the world is but the history of His influence and that the center of the whole universe is the cross of Calvary."

However *you've* thought about Jesus in the past, I hope you'll join me in thinking about Him again.

Christmas and Easter

People who only go to church at Christmas and Easter are sometimes known, somewhat unkindly, as "Chreasters." We do think about Jesus at these times. At Christmastime, we buy the presents, set up the tree, and celebrate His birth. Our presents are emblematic of the gift God gave us in His Son, and they also recall perhaps the gifts brought to the Christ child by the Magi, the three wise men from the East who were present at His birth.

During Easter, we celebrate Jesus's resurrection from the dead. Crucified by the Romans (handed over to them by Jewish officials), Jesus is entombed until what was to become Easter morning. On that morning, women going to the tomb to anoint His body discover the empty tomb and report back to His followers that Jesus has risen. An angel says to the women first approaching the tomb that morning, "Why do you look for the living among the dead?" (Luke 24:5).

As you think about Jesus and Christianity, stop right here and be sure you understand something. Jesus of Nazareth was crucified, dead, on a Roman cross; he was entombed, and three days later he rose from the dead. This is a fact. To say otherwise requires solid proof, and, as Lee Strobel and others have made clear, there is no other plausible explanation.

Many of us have heard these things about Jesus for much of our lives, but perhaps the overall impact of Jesus on life as we've come to know is not so familiar to you. Allow me the point that Schaff makes above, that the influence of Jesus is incalculable.

In this chapter, I include a basic summary of the events of Jesus's life from the Bible. Again, this is a story you may already know, but some of you, however, may not know it, and for you, I thought it important to establish a threshold level of knowledge of Jesus's life.

As we proceed, as I said a moment ago, remember that I present the information about Jesus as fact. I understand that you yourself may not accept it as such. I ask that you allow me this position for now for the purpose just mentioned: to establish a basic understanding of the information we have surrounding Jesus's life.

Jesus's Birth and Early Years

I actually begin this section before Jesus's birth, by talking about His mother, Mary, and the manner of Jesus's conception. This is the Gospel writer Luke's account:

> In the sixth month of Elizabeth's [cousin of Mary; mother of John the Baptist] pregnancy, God sent the

> angel Gabriel to Nazareth, a town in Galilee, to a virgin pledged to be married to a man named Joseph, a descendant of David. The virgin's name was Mary. The angel went to her and said, "Greetings, you who are highly favored! The Lord is with you." (Luke 1:26–28)

Mary, of course, is startled by her visitor, especially when she hears that she is to have a Son, and such a Son! Gabriel says that the Son "will be great, and will be called the Son of the most High. The Lord God will give Him the throne of His father David ... and He will reign over Jacob's descendants forever" (Luke 1:32–35).

There's one small hitch that Mary sees and communicates to Gabriel. "How will this be," Mary asked the angel, "since I am a virgin?" (Luke 1:34).

Gabriel responds, "The Holy Spirit will come upon you, and the power of the Highest will overshadow you; therefore, also, that Holy One who is to be born will be called the Son of God" (Luke 1:35). Gabriel tells Mary that nothing is impossible with God, reminding her that her relative Elizabeth had also recently conceived.

To all of this, Mary responds, "I am the Lord's servant. May your word to me be fulfilled" (Luke 1:38). With this, the angel departs. Shortly after, the Holy Spirit does visit Mary as described, and Jesus is conceived.

Luke tells us that Jesus is preceded in birth by John, the son just alluded to of Elizabeth and her husband Zacharias. As we just saw, this is the John who later becomes John the Baptist. As we will see, John becomes the "voice crying in the wilderness," announcing the coming of the Chosen One. The prophets of the Old Testament had foretold that God would send a Messiah to relieve the Jews of their bondage, and Jesus is the One of whom John the Baptist speaks.

A Celebratory Birth

When Mary visits Elizabeth, we read that the yet-unborn John "leaped in her womb" and learn that the unborn baby had done this previously upon Elizabeth's hearing that Mary was also with child. John is apparently aware of his mission before he actually comes into the world.

You probably recall the familiar stories surrounding Jesus's birth. Joseph and Mary were obliged to travel to Bethlehem (Joseph's birthplace) to register in response to a decree from Caesar Augustus. As Mary's time to deliver approached, they sought lodging in Bethlehem, but all the inns were full, so they were forced to lodge in a stable. When Jesus was born, we hear that He was placed in "swaddling clothes" and laid in a manger (a small trough in which animal feed was placed).

At Jesus's birth, we read that an angel appeared to shepherds in the fields nearby, saying, "Do not be afraid. I bring you good news that will cause great joy for all the people. Today in the town of David a Savior has been born to you; He is the Messiah, the Lord. This will be a sign to you: You will find a baby wrapped in cloths lying in a manger" (Luke 2:11–12) The shepherds "came with haste" and found the baby in the manger, as the angel had proclaimed.

Others came to the manger as well, wise men from the east who had followed the star to Bethlehem; they brought gold and other gifts to honor Jesus.

All of these events are recounted in scripture and in hymns familiar to most of us: "Joy to the World" and "Silent Night, Holy Night," to name only two.

As a baby, Jesus was brought to Jerusalem so that Mary and Joseph could "present Him to the Lord" (Luke 2:22). Here, another singular thing happens. At this time, a man named Simeon, "just and devout," had been waiting in Jerusalem for "the Consolation of Israel," or the coming of the long-awaited Messiah. We hear that "the Holy Spirit was upon him."

As Jesus is brought forward for the ceremony, Simeon takes Him and says that he has now seen enough in his lifetime:

> For my eyes have seen Your salvation,
> which you have prepared in the sight of all nations:
> A light for revelation to the Gentiles,
> and the glory of your people Israel. (Luke 2:30–32)

If you are not familiar with the term "Gentile," it refers to any person who is not Jewish. Simeon tells Mary that Jesus is destined "for the fall and rising of many in Israel"—that He is, in other words, the Chosen One the Jews had been praying for and expecting.

Anna, "a prophetess," was also there at the time that Jesus was presented and also greeted Jesus as the Redeemer: "She gave thanks to God, and spoke about the child to all who were looking for the redemption of Jerusalem" (Luke 2:38).

Royal Visitors

If you are familiar with Jesus's birth story, you recall that the wise men came to see Him, that angels were singing, that the shepherds came in from the fields to see Him, that as you just saw, prophets paid homage, that Jesus was to bring "salvation" to His people, to lead them, it would seem, into a new Eden.

Well, that didn't happen. We can ask understandably, "What happened *next*?" The Gospel stories don't tell us. In Gospel accounts, we hear about His birth, the visit of the Magi, the angels singing on high, the shepherds coming in from the fields—then nothing for a dozen years or so.

This is a problem for me! Choirs of angels sang, shepherds gathered, wise men appeared bearing gifts—and then nothing of real substance happens in scripture until we see Jesus begin His ministry as an adult! What gives?

Here is my less-than-satisfactory explanation. Even in adulthood, Jesus says to His mother at one point, "My time has not yet come." As a boy and as a young man, this would also have been true, and since His time (meaning the ministry He would engage in and the sacrifice He would make) in fact *had* not come, the Gospel writers apparently did not consider the intervening years significant enough to include. They were led by the Spirit to include what they included, and that's what they did.

The only event we do hear of concerning Jesus's boyhood occurred when He was twelve years old, when Mary and Joseph took Him to

Jerusalem for the Feast of the Passover. In what may be a sign of negligent parenting, Mary and Joseph traveled a full day toward home after the feast, without realizing that Jesus wasn't with them (Luke says they thought He was with others "in the company").

It takes them three days to find Him, and when they do, they discover Him in the temple, "sitting among the teachers, listening to them and asking them questions. Everyone who heard him was amazed at his understanding and his answers" (Luke 2:46–47).

Mary told Him that she and His father had been anxiously searching for Him. "Why were you searching for me?" he asked. "Didn't you know that I had to be in my Father's house?" (Luke 2:49). We are told that His parents "did not understand what he was saying to them" (Luke 2:50).

We learn much later that Joseph and Mary had other children in later years, but the Gospel writers tell us little about them.

John the Baptist

Recall that Elizabeth had been with child at the same time that Mary was—that her baby, who was to be John, had been "leaping" in her womb in excitement over Mary's child.

John was to be the one who "prepared the way" for Jesus. In the Gospels, he simply appears in the region of the Jordan River, preaching repentance "for the remission of sins." John was the fulfillment of the prophecy of Isaiah:

> A voice of one calling:
> "In the wilderness
> prepare the way for the Lord;
> make straight in the desert
> a highway for our God." (Isaiah 40:3)

We hear a good deal in the Gospel stories about prophecies needing to be fulfilled. Old Testament prophets, perhaps especially Isaiah, foretold of the coming of the Messiah. There would be both

Jewish and Gentile (non-Jewish) people to whom the good news of Jesus would be preached, and those doing the preaching (including Jesus Himself) knew how important it was to establish Jesus's ministry as part of this larger story. John, as you just saw, identifies himself as the one "crying in the wilderness" for people to repent, knowing how this would resonate with his Jewish audience.

John believed in a "less is more" approach to apparel and diet, choosing animal skins for his clothing and locusts and wild honey for part of his diet. He was not kind to the religious leaders who came to hear him, saying at one point, "You brood of vipers! Who warned you to flee from the coming wrath? Produce fruit in keeping with repentance. And do not begin to say to yourselves, 'We have Abraham as our father.' For I tell you that out of these stones God can raise up children for Abraham" (Luke 3:7–8).

John precedes Jesus in telling all he preaches to that a new day is coming. The Jews were very well versed in the law, the Torah that we described in the last chapter, and all its rules for staying right with God. This led to what John and later Jesus saw as too great an emphasis on those rules and too little care for what was in people's hearts. After He began His ministry, Jesus was to have many debates with the scribes and the Pharisees, two groups within the Jewish faith who achieved status through recording and interpreting the law.

Tellingly, given that Jesus is about to begin His ministry, John says to the "brood of vipers" referenced above, "The ax is already at the root of the trees, and every tree that does not bear good fruit will be cut down and thrown into the fire" (Luke 3:9).

It is John who baptizes Jesus. John says of Jesus, "After me comes the one more powerful than I, the straps of whose sandals I am not worthy to stoop down and untie. I baptized you with water, but He will baptize you with the Holy Spirit" (Mark 1:7–8).

Luke's Gospel recounts these same words of John, but adds, "He will baptize you with the Holy Spirit and fire. His winnowing fork is in His hand, to clear His threshing floor, and to gather the wheat into His barn, but He will burn up the chaff with unquenchable fire" (Luke 3:16–17).

At the moment of Jesus's baptism, John says poignantly to Him, "I need to be baptized by You, and do you come to me?" (Matthew 3:14). Jesus tells John, "Let it to be so now; it is proper for us to do this to fulfill all righteousness" (Matthew 3:15).

Jesus says this because the baptizing John was doing was for people repenting of their sins, and Jesus, as the Son of God, was sinless. It is thought that Jesus submitted to baptism by John to join ranks with those renewing their faith through John, to thus validate the ministry of John and to fulfill the will of His Father.

The message of John is that the people of the time, including the "broods of vipers," had not walked the straight and narrow in terms of being right with God and that, with the coming of Jesus, they had best mend their ways. God was about to affect their lives in a very different way than He had in the past. He had arrived in the flesh.

Tempted by the Devil

In the Gospels, we read that following His baptism, Jesus is taken into the desert for forty days and tempted by the devil. The devil is Lucifer, once an angel and one of God's favorites, but now cast into hell for leading a rebellion against the Lord. In the first letter of Peter in the New Testament, Peter gives this description: "Be alert and of sober mind. Your enemy the devil prowls around like a roaring lion, looking for someone to devour" (1 Peter 5:8).

He indeed sought to "devour" Jesus in the desert, tempting Him to abandon His ministry. Jesus was fasting, and we hear that He was hungry. The devil says to him, "If you are the Son of God, tell these stones to become bread" (Matthew 4:3). Jesus responds with the familiar "It is written: 'Man shall not live on bread alone, but by every word that comes from the mouth of God'" (Matthew 4:4).

The devil then asks Jesus to verify His superhuman powers, if I may call them that. He takes Jesus "to the pinnacle of the temple" and says to Him, "If you are the Son of God, throw yourself down. For it is written:

'He will command His angels concerning you,
and they will lift you up in their hands,
So that you will not strike your foot against a stone.'"
(Matthew 4:6)

But Jesus is having none of it. He says, "It is also written: 'Do not put the Lord your God to the test" (Matthew 4:7).

The devil then plays his last card, taking Jesus up "to a very high mountain" and showing Him "all the kingdoms of the world and their splendor. 'All this I will give you,' he said, 'if you will fall down and worship me'" (Matthew 4:8–9).

Jesus says, "Away from me, Satan! For it is written: 'Worship the Lord your God, and serve him only" (Matthew 4:10).

With this the devil gives up. Jesus soon leaves Nazareth and Galilee, and dwells for a time in Capernaum. Here He begins the three-year ministry that will culminate in His Crucifixion, death, and resurrection.

When Were the Gospels Written?

The grille of a 1946 Chevrolet was in the shape of a half-oval. I guess the object it resembles most closely is a protractor of the type we used in grade school. The straight side of the grille was aligned horizontally with the car's front bumper, and the rest curved up from that. There were three horizontal bars parallel to the front bumper that extended across the grille.

In 1947, the shape of the grille remained the same, but Chevrolet decided to extend the horizontal bars outside of the grille—so the smooth arc of the grille from the 1946 model was disrupted.

The grille of the 1946 Chevrolet is only one detail that I remember. The first 1946 Chevy I saw was in our front driveway. Its appearance there, I was to learn later, was quite a momentous event, because it reflected the fact that American industry was once again in full swing, manufacturing products for domestic use versus war use. The one my dad drove home was tan and brown. It was a four-door sedan, tan on the bottom with a brown top. It did not have seat belts, and its radio was simple enough that a normal person could understand it.

I actually saw this car in 1946, coming up on seventy-four years ago. I know; you didn't realize you were reading someone this old. I'm old but still somewhat wiry and agile.

I remember exactly what I was doing on November 22, 1963 when President Kennedy was assassinated. I was going into the Student Union at Western Washington State College (now Western Washington University) in Bellingham, Washington. My friend, Dennis Koeppen, from Longview, Washington, whom I'd known since grade school, was near the door, and instead of responding to my cheerful greeting, Dennis said, "President Kennedy's been shot." This occurred fifty-seven years ago.

In neither of the two instances recounted can anyone dispute me, because I have the concrete memory of my own experience. I was there; I know what happened. I saw, touched, and sat in the 1946 Chevy. I saw the shock on Dennis's face, and saw that he was crying.

The Gospel of Matthew is dated by scholars between 50 and 60 CE. This places the book twenty to thirty years after Jesus's crucifixion. The Gospels of Mark and Luke are dated somewhat later, in the 60s. John, the latest Gospel, is thought to have been written in the late 80s to early 90s. *This places the most recent Gospel of Jesus no later than sixty years after His death in approximately 30—approximately the number of years between my experience of the 1946 Chevrolet and the present moment.*

I make the comparison between events of my life and those recounted in the Gospels to make this point: The Gospel stories aren't legends. They weren't written hundreds of years after the fact, years that would blur the historical facts and erase potentially conflicting testimony from others with firsthand knowledge. Other New Testament documents can also be dated very closely to the events they describe.

I wanted to make this point before we continue our account of Jesus's life—to reinforce the point that the Gospel writers knew whereof they spoke. They spoke from firsthand, carefully considered experience.

Jesus's Ministry

The actual events of Jesus's mission are fairly easy to recount. He chose His disciples, the twelve men who came to comprise his inner circle, men who learned from Him and who spread His message both during His lifetime and after His death. He traveled in a fairly small circle in Palestine, teaching, preaching, healing, and performing other miracles. He was challenged by the Jewish religious establishment, which sought to discredit Him.

He was hugely popular, often preaching to multitudes, which caused consternation among both the Jewish religious authorities and the Romans who governed the provinces. He was finally betrayed by one of His disciples, Judas Iscariot, and the Jewish authorities arrested Him and handed Him over to the Romans for punishment. Pontius Pilate, the Roman procurator, initially found that Jesus had committed no crime, but yielded to public pressure instigated by the Jews and condemned Jesus to punishment and then death by crucifixion. Jesus was crucified between two criminals at Golgotha (the "Place of the Skull") in Jerusalem.

He was buried in the tomb of Joseph of Arimathea, a Jewish leader who, according to Matthew, "had also become a disciple of Jesus" (Matthew 27:57). He rose three days later, appeared to His disciples and others a number of times, and finally ascended again to the Father, vowing to be with His followers "to the very end of the age" (Matthew 28:20).

Let's comment a bit more fully now on each of these areas of His life and ministry.

What was Jesus's mission? According to the Gospel of Luke, Jesus announces this very early in His ministry. Shortly after He was tempted by the devil, Jesus went to the synagogue in Nazareth on Sabbath Day and stood up to read. He was handed the book of the prophet Isaiah, opened it, and read aloud the following passage:

> The Spirit of the Lord is on me,
> because he has anointed me
> to proclaim the good news to the poor.

> He has sent me to proclaim freedom for the
> prisoners
> and recovery of sight for the blind,
> to set the oppressed free,
> to proclaim the year of the Lord's favor. (Luke 4:18–19)

Then we read this extraordinary passage: "Then he rolled up the scroll, gave it back to the attendant and sat down. The eyes of everyone in the synagogue were fastened on Him. He began by saying to them, 'Today this scripture is fulfilled in your hearing'" (Luke 4:20–21).

Since He was speaking to people who had known Him since He was a boy, the people were "furious when they heard this" and "drove him out of the town." They even attempted to kill Him, "but he walked right through the crowd and went on his way" (Luke 4:30).

We can't comprehend how shocking Jesus's announcement would have been to the people in attendance. The Jews had been waiting for the promised Messiah for hundreds of years. Their lives were carefully prescribed by tradition—what to wear, what to eat, when to pray, how to pray—and to hear that Joseph's son, Jesus, the local carpenter, was in fact the Chosen One they'd been waiting for would simply be too much for them to accept.

This passage is critical in light of what Jesus does in the three years of His ministry. He does preach the Gospel (the good news of salvation) to the poor; He does heal, both the "brokenhearted" and those with all manner of physical ailments; He does "proclaim liberty to the captives," although it's often a liberating of the spirit as opposed to the body; and He does provide sight to the blind, both those who are physically blind and those who are blind in the spiritual sense.

The Disciples

The Gospel writers vary somewhat in their descriptions of how Jesus recruits His twelve disciples. Here is Matthew's account of how Jesus enlists Simon (later called Peter) and his brother Andrew, both of whom were Galilean fishermen:

> They were casting their net into the lake.... "Come follow Me," Jesus said, "and I will send you out to fish for people." At once they left their nets and followed Him. (Matthew 4:18–20)

Luke's account is somewhat different. In his version, Simon and Andrew had been fishing without success, close to where Jesus had been preaching. Jesus actually preaches from Simon's (Peter's) boat, while Simon and Andrew wash their nets. When He finishes preaching, He invites Simon and Andrew to come with Him, pushing out into some deeper water, to continue fishing.

Peter (I'll use this name from now on) is reluctant, saying that they'd tried all morning without success, but in deference to Jesus, he agrees. They catch so many fish that their boat begins to sink, and they are obliged to get two of their partners (Luke's term) to come help them, and they too load their boat to the limit with fish.

The two partners are James and John, sons of Zebedee. Luke's version of Jesus's invitation to His first four disciples is "Do not be afraid. From now on you will fish for people" (Luke 5:10). Here is the startling conclusion: "So they pulled their boats up on shore, left everything and followed him" (Luke 5:11).

In Matthew's account, James and John are actually in their boat with their father, Zebedee, mending nets. When Jesus calls them, they "immediately left the boat and their father, and followed Him" (Matthew 4:22).

All of them "forsook all and followed Him." We can imagine poor Zebedee's consternation when his two sons leave him in the boat (one could say "in the lurch") and walk away with Jesus. Something in Jesus's manner and speech compels them to follow Him.

In similar ways, He recruits the rest of His inner circle. Perhaps one of His more controversial selections is Matthew, the tax collector. In Luke, we read, "After this, Jesus went out and saw a tax collector named Levi, sitting at his tax booth. 'Follow me,' Jesus said to him, and Levi got up, left everything and followed him" (Luke 5:27–28).

We are told that Levi (Matthew) arranges a feast for Jesus, "and a large crowd of tax collectors and others were eating with them" (Luke

5:29). The ever vigilant (and ever suspicious) scribes and Pharisees take issue with this, asking Jesus, "Why do you eat and drink with tax collectors and sinners?" (Luke 5:30).

Jesus's response is, "It is not the healthy who need a doctor, but the sick. I have not come to call the righteous, but sinners to repentance" (Luke 5:31–32).

This passage is revealing in that it reinforces Jesus's announced mission (to call sinners to repentance) and in what it says about the caliber of people Jesus selects to assist Him in ministry.

Having been raised in it and studied it, Jesus was steeped in Jewish religious tradition. He was surrounded by learned rabbis (teachers) and the aforementioned scribes, Pharisees, and perhaps even more conservative Sadducees (the latter held that only the first five books of the Old Testament, the Torah, held God's revealed truth).

So we could ask, understandably, why not choose some of these to assist him? They would have neither the learning curve of poor fishermen nor people's distaste for the tax collector to work through. They could speak with eloquence and force. Why not them?

I think the answer lies in Jesus's comment about whom He came to call. He wanted to reach the poor, the afflicted, the downcast. While the disciples may not have exhibited all of these qualities, their humble origins and occupations made them more suited to Jesus's ministry to the region's have-nots. He was to call His disciples later "the salt of the earth," and that they were.

So off they went. Jesus and the twelve preached and taught in the region of Galilee and Judea for the next three years. You may have heard about the miracles. At a wedding feast, Jesus turns water into wine. At a gathering of more than five thousand, Jesus feeds all of them with just five loaves of bread and two fish. When they were finished, Luke says, "They all ate and were satisfied, and the disciples picked up twelve basketfuls of broken pieces that were left over" (Luke 9:17).

He returns sight to the blind. He cleanses lepers. A woman "who had been subject to bleeding for twelve years" (Luke 8:43) simply touches Jesus's garment as He passes and is healed of her condition. He casts out demons and evil spirits. He raises people from the dead.

In the most dramatic of the latter cases, Jesus raises Lazarus, brother of Mary and Martha, from the dead. We meet Mary and Martha as dedicated followers of Jesus, well before the story of Lazarus. Jesus had known of Lazarus's illness but did not go to him until Lazarus had been in his tomb for four days. Of this, Jesus says, "This sickness will not end in death. No, it is for God's glory so that God's son may be glorified through it" (John 11:4).

Told by Martha that Lazarus is already dead, Jesus says, "I am the resurrection and the life. The one who believes in me will live, even though they die; and whoever lives by believing in me will never die. Do you believe this?" (John 11:25–26).

Jesus goes to Lazarus' tomb. "'But Lord,' said Martha, the sister of the dead man, 'by this time there is a bad odor, for he has been there four days'" (John 11:39).

Then Jesus lifts His eyes heavenward and prays, "Father, I thank you that you have heard me. And I knew that You always hear me, but I said this for the benefit of the people standing here, that they may believe that you sent me" (John 11:41–42). Jesus then says in a loud voice, "Lazarus, come forth."

Lazarus emerges from the tomb, "his hands and feet wrapped with strips of linen, and a cloth around his face" (John 11:44).

Despite His popularity—in part due to the kinds of miracles just described—the forces that would destroy Jesus's earthly ministry gradually closed in on Him. Shortly after He raised Lazarus from the dead, He does enter Jerusalem in triumph on what has come to be called Palm Sunday, but that success is soon eclipsed by His arrest, trial, and crucifixion.

The Jewish priests conspire with Judas in the arrest of Jesus, after which He is brought before the Jewish high council (Sanhedrin) for trial. What seals Jesus's fate at the hands of Caiaphas, the high priest, is His answer to this direct question: "I charge you under oath by the living God: Tell us if you are the Messiah, the Son of God" (Matthew 26:63).

Jesus says, "You have said so. But I say to all of you: From now on you will see the Son of Man sitting at the right hand of the Mighty One and coming on the clouds of heaven" (John 26:64).

This is considered blasphemy and cause for death. Jesus is beaten, spat upon, and turned over to the Romans (only the Roman governors could carry out a sentence of death). It was all as Jesus had foretold. Matthew records Jesus saying:

> We are going up to Jerusalem, and the Son of Man will be delivered over to the chief priests and the teachers of the law. They will condemn him to death and will hand him over to the Gentiles to be mocked and flogged and crucified. On the third day he will be raised to life. (Matthew 20:18–19)

Crucifixion was the most horrific death possible during Jesus's time (or perhaps any time). It was reserved for the lowest kind of criminals and was the most excruciating death imaginable, with some victims lingering for days on their crosses. This is what Jesus knew His fate to be, and He accepted it willingly, saying, "The Son of Man did not come to be served, but to serve, and to give His life as a ransom for many" (Matthew 20:28).

Luke says that Jesus, dying on the cross, said, "Father, forgive them, for they do not know what they are doing" (Luke 23:34).

With His death on the cross, the biggest part of Jesus's earthly mission was accomplished. His Crucifixion occurred on what has become called Good Friday. Jesus's body is taken and placed in the tomb of Joseph of Arimathea, the disciple referred to earlier.

The Jewish chief priests and Pharisees remembered that Jesus had said that He would rise in three days, so they returned to Pilate and asked that a guard be placed at the tomb, "Otherwise his disciples may come and steal the body and tell the people that he has been raised from the dead" (Matthew 27:64). Accordingly, a large stone was placed at the entrance of the tomb.

Here is how Mark describes the discovery of the empty tomb on the third day:

> When the Sabbath was over, Mary Magdalene, Mary the mother of James, and Salome bought spices so that they might go to anoint Jesus' body. Very early on

> the first day of the week, just after sunrise, they were on their way to the tomb and they asked each other, "Who will roll the stone away from the entrance of the tomb?"
>
> But when they looked up, they saw that the stone, which was very large, had been rolled away. As they entered the tomb, they saw a young man dressed in a white robe sitting on the right side, and they were alarmed.
>
> "Don't be alarmed," he said. "You are looking for Jesus the Nazarene, who was crucified. He has risen! He is not here. See the place where they laid him. But go, and tell his disciples and Peter, 'He is going ahead of you into Galilee. There you will see him, just as he told you.'" (Mark 16:1–7)

They did see Him and received His promise of the Holy Spirit, the Comforter, Who would be with them until His return.

This brief summary of the events of Jesus's life establishes a context for our next chapter, which delves more deeply into the content of Jesus's ministry.

Chapter Five

Jesus's Ministry

On my account you will be brought before governors and kings as witnesses to them and to the Gentiles. But when they arrest you, do not worry about what to say or how to say it. At that time you will be given what to say, for it will not be you speaking, but the Spirit of your Father speaking through you. (Matthew 10:18–20)

New Birth

Nicodemus was no dummy. John tells us that he was "a member of the Jewish ruling council" (John 3:1). The Pharisees focused on exacting interpretations of Jewish law. We give them credit for trying to do God's bidding by studying and clarifying the law. This is doubtless behind Nicodemus's visit to Jesus.

There was tension between Jesus and the Pharisees. For the Pharisees, "righteousness" was obtained through keeping the law; for Jesus, righteousness was obtained through having faith. It was dangerous for Pharisees to associate too closely with Jesus, and for this reason, we hear that Nicodemus comes to Jesus "by night." He tells Jesus, "Rabbi, we know that you are a teacher who has come from God. For no one could perform the signs [miracles] you are doing if God were not with Him" (John 3:1–2).

Jesus replied, "Very truly I tell you, no one can see the kingdom of God unless they are born again" (John 3:3).

Nicodemus doesn't understand this: "How can someone be born when they are old?' Nicodemus asked. 'Surely they cannot enter a second time into their mother's womb to be born'" (John 3:4). (From this, you get just a hint of the literalism that affected the Pharisees.)

Jesus explains:

> Very truly I tell you, no one can enter the kingdom of God unless they are born of water and the Spirit. Flesh gives birth to flesh, but the Spirit gives birth to spirit. You should not be surprised at my saying, "You must be born again." The wind blows wherever it pleases. You hear its sound, but you cannot tell where it comes from or where it is going. So it is with everyone born of the Spirit. (John 3:5–8)

We will return to the encounter between Nicodemus and Jesus in a moment.

Riches and the Kingdom of Heaven

Shortly before Jesus's triumphant entry into Jerusalem on Palm Sunday, Luke tells us of His encounter with "a certain ruler." This individual says to Jesus, "Good Teacher, what must I do to inherit eternal life?" (Luke 18:18).

Jesus says that he must keep the commandments: do not commit adultery, do not murder, do not bear false witness, and so on. The young gentleman says, "All these things I have kept since I was a boy." Jesus answers, "You still lack one thing. Sell everything you have and give to the poor, and you will have treasure in heaven. Then come, follow Me" (Luke 18:22).

Luke then says of the young man, "When he heard this he became very sad, for he was very wealthy" (Luke 18:23).

Jesus too becomes sorrowful at this point, saying, "How hard it is for the rich to enter the kingdom of God! Indeed, it is easier for a camel to go through the eye of a needle than for someone who is rich to enter the kingdom of God" (Luke 18:24–25).

The Woman at the Well

Early in the Gospel of John, we read of Jesus's encounter with "a woman of Samaria." This encounter is important on several levels.

The first is that the Samaritan woman is that: a woman. Women held little status in Jesus's time, yet they are featured prominently in the Gospels. As we saw in the last chapter, it was to be women who discovered Jesus's empty tomb and who brought the good news of His resurrection to the disciples.

The second important fact of Jesus's encounter with the Samaritan woman is that she is from Samaria. The Jews had long considered the Samaritans "impure." When this region was occupied by the Assyrians during what was called "the Exile," intermarriage eventually occurred between Jews and Samaritans, leading to the impurity of the resulting generations. Thus, any contact between Jews and Samaritans was to be minimized.

We can read additional significance into this encounter because not only is it the meeting place between Jesus, a Jew, and the Samaritan woman, but it occurs at the well that had belonged to Jacob, which he had bequeathed to Joseph hundreds of years earlier. There is thus considerable biblical weight to the setting in which Jesus and the woman meet.

And finally, their meeting is important because of what the woman is to learn of the tired, hungry, thirsty individual she encounters. Here is what happens:

John first sets the scene, saying, "Jacob's well was there, and Jesus, tired as he was from the journey, sat down by the well. It was about noon" (John 4:6).

Jesus is by Himself, the disciples having gone off to buy food. Jesus asks the woman for a drink from the well.

The woman responds, "You are a Jew and I am a Samaritan woman. How can you ask me for a drink?" John reminds us, "For Jews do not associate with Samaritans" (John 4:9). Jesus answers, "If you knew the gift of God and who it is who asks you for a drink, you would have asked Him, and he would have given you living water" (John 4:10).

The woman complains that Jesus has nothing to draw with, and asks him further where he expects to find this "living water," asking if Jesus thinks he's greater than "our father Jacob, who gave us the well, and drank from it himself, as did his sons and his livestock?" (John 4:11–12).

Jesus responds, "Everyone who drinks this water will be thirsty again, but whoever drinks the water I give them will never thirst. Indeed, the water I give him will become in them a spring of water welling up into eternal life" (John 4:13–14).

The woman asks for some of this water, but Jesus instead asks her to go and call her husband to join them. When she responds that she has no husband, Jesus startles her by saying, "You have had five husbands, and the man you now have is not your husband. What you have just said is quite true" (John 4:18).

The woman recognizes then that Jesus is a prophet, which leads her to say, "Our ancestors worshiped on this mountain, but you Jews claim that the place where we must worship is in Jerusalem" (John 4:20).

Jesus replies:

> Woman ... believe me, a time is coming when you will worship the father neither on this mountain nor in Jerusalem. You Samaritans worship what you do not know; we worship what we do know, for salvation is from the Jews. Yet a time is coming and has now come when the true worshippers will worship the Father in Spirit and in truth, for they are the kind of worshippers the Father seeks. God is Spirit, and his worshippers must worship in the Spirit and in truth. (John 4:21–24)

The woman says, "I know that Messiah" (called Christ) "is coming. When He comes, He will explain everything to us" (John 4:25).

Jesus responds, "I, the one speaking to you—I am he" (John 4:26).

The Kingdom of God

Nicodemus, the learned Pharisee. The rich young ruler. The Samaritan woman at Jacob's well. Let's look at these three encounters in more detail and try to discover what Jesus is getting at in each.

Remember from the last chapter that Jesus tipped His hand, as it were, in His home village of Nazareth:

> The Spirit of the Lord is on me,
> because He has anointed me
> to proclaim good news to the poor.
> He has sent me to proclaim freedom for the prisoners
> and recovery of sight for the blind,
> to set the oppressed free,
> to proclaim the year of the Lord's favor.
> (Luke 4:18–19)

And Luke tells us, "Then he rolled up the scroll, gave it back to the attendant and sat down. The eyes of all who were in the synagogue were fastened on Him. He began by saying to them, 'Today this scripture is fulfilled in your hearing'" (Luke 4:20–21).

Knowing what we know of the culture of that time, it is little wonder that the people who heard Jesus say this drove Him out of the synagogue and tried to kill him. He had said to them that He was the One, the One John the Baptist said "will baptize you with the Holy Spirit and with fire" (Luke 3:11).

The Jews had been expecting a mighty warrior, another King David, who would restore their former status and defeat their oppressors. And here is Jesus, the carpenter, telling them that He is the One.

As we consider the reaction of the Jews in the synagogue to what

Jesus said, remember that their faith wasn't simply a collection of ideas to them. Their faith was woven into every facet of their lives. In our culture, we may go to church on Sunday. We might serve on a committee. We might go to Sunday school. The rest of the time, we can pretty much do what we want.

Not so for the Jews. Virtually every part of their lives was affected by their religion: what food to prepare, how to prepare that food, when to work, when not to work, when to cover your head, when not to cover your head, what did the law say, how did it say it, who can interpret for us, what can occur on the Sabbath and what can't, and so on.

Their lives were a tapestry of these connected strands of belief and conduct. And during Jesus's time, their deliverance from the Romans was to be accomplished by the return of the Chosen One, the Messiah. With God's help, He would sweep the Romans away, and the Jews would return to enlightened self-rule under God.

But Jesus, the mild-mannered carpenter's son? What on earth was He talking about?

What Jesus was talking about was the Kingdom of God. When He told His neighbors that He had come to "proclaim the acceptable year of the Lord," He was saying "This is it, and I'm It." The time had come. It's little wonder that they recoiled in disbelief and then angrily tried to kill him.

Poor Nicodemus couldn't understand Him. Nicodemus couldn't grasp the "unless a man be born again" part. I don't think we get that part, either, but it appears that Jesus was inviting Nicodemus, the rich young ruler, and the woman at the well into a new reality, one achieved, as Saint Paul was to say in his letter to the church in Rome, by "the renewing of your mind" (Romans 12:2).

Life in the Kingdom

Jesus said to Nicodemus, "That which is born of flesh is flesh, and that which is born of spirit is Spirit. Do not marvel that I said to you, 'You must be born again.'" He tells Nicodemus that he must be born into the life of the spirit. Remember this passage, the part that says, "That which is born of flesh is flesh."

To the rich young ruler, Jesus says that he must sell all his possessions, "give to the poor," and come follow Him. Is this the same message? In essence, it is. Jesus is saying that a new reality, a new kingdom, is here, one that has nothing to do with things of the flesh—including wealth and possessions. In His Sermon on the Mount, Jesus tells His audience:

> Do not lay up for yourselves treasures on earth, where moths and vermin destroy, and where thieves break in and steal. But store up for yourselves treasures in heaven, where moths and vermin do not destroy, and where thieves do not break in and steal. For where your treasure is, there your heart will be also. (Matthew 6:19–21)

And He says to the woman at the well:

> You Samaritans worship what you do not know; we worship what we do know, for salvation is from the Jews. Yet a time is coming and has now come when the true worshipers will worship the Father in spirit and truth; for they are the kind of worshipers the Father seeks. God is Spirit, and his worshipers must worship in the Spirit and in truth. (John 4:21–24)

That which is born of the flesh is flesh, and as He told Nicodemus, unless we worship God in Spirit, we can't enter His kingdom. Unless the rich young ruler gives up his possessions, he can't enter the kingdom of God. To the woman at the well, he says, "God is Spirit, and his worshipers must worship in the Spirit and in truth."

New Life in the Spirit

Jesus offered Nicodemus, the rich young ruler, and the woman at the well a new life. It is so shockingly new that often He couldn't speak of it directly but spoke instead in parables to make clear what He meant. The new life that He offers is what makes Jesus leap out of the pages of the New Testament. No one has said the things Jesus said. No one has ever asked of His followers what Jesus asks of them: to be reborn in the spirit.

What we as human beings fear perhaps more than anything is death. In our country, we live in a culture that glorifies and tries to prolong youth. Our culture places a high value on physical beauty and physical strength. We place a high value on materiality. We like food and clothes and shoes and cars and boats and houses. We adore and are enslaved by technology: laptops, iPads, Siri, and smartphones that do everything except clean our ears. We see bumper stickers that read "He who dies with the most toys wins." In short, we like—thrive on—technology and materiality.

We are enclosed by and are identified to quite a degree by our bodies. When you think about it, the items mentioned in the last paragraph are mainly elaborate extensions of our bodies. Clothes are extensions of our skin. Cars, motorcycles, trucks, boats, bicycles, and skateboards are extensions of our feet and legs—our means of locomotion. Electronics are extensions of our eyes, ears, and voices (i.e., cameras for sight, iPods for hearing, and media in general for our voices—I can speak through a website, a blog, a webinar). Houses are extensions of our entire bodies. They encase us, the same way our bodies do.

Jesus would say that all of these things are "of the flesh." Some relate to our actual flesh directly (e.g., food), and some comprise the extensions identified above. Of course, God understands that we need some of these things:

> So do not worry, saying "What shall we eat?" or "What shall we drink?" or "What shall we wear?" For the pagans run after all these things, and your heavenly father knows that you need them. But seek first his kingdom and his righteousness, and all these things will be given to you as well. (Matthew 6:31–33)

What Jesus offers is *escape* from materiality. The escape is in the form of relief from worry (over all the material issues that confront us), and it is also in the form of actual victory over death itself, because Jesus overcame death. Let me say that again: *Jesus overcame death.* He brought others back from death to life, and He Himself rose from the dead. That is the shocking truth.

Life in the Body

How can we characterize the dual nature of our makeup? The "flesh," as Jesus and Paul refer to it, versus the spirit? Our culture seems to lean heavily toward the flesh. In the absence of intellectual or spiritual interests, and given the immediate pleasures that can accrue when we engage the flesh, this seems obvious and understandable. Attending to the demands of the body leads to immediate satisfaction and pleasure, but these are short-lived actions that require repetition as well as greater and greater intensity. As answers to what our lives ultimately mean, they are inadequate and shallow.

As we will see below, Paul refuses to accept an artificial dichotomy of flesh and spirit. We are single entities made up of complementary and reinforcing systems, and God is at work in all of them.

Delmore Schwarz wrote a poem that expresses the opposite view. He characterizes his body as "The Heavy Bear That Goes with Me" in a poem having that title—definitely separating the "bear" of his sensuous nature with what we could call our higher intellectual and spiritual selves. In his "Heavy Bear" poem, he emphasizes that he is *not* his body; rather, his body is this heavy bear who is always with him:

> That inescapable animal walks with me,
> Has followed me since the black womb held,
> Moves where I move, distorting my gesture,
> A caricature, a swollen shadow,
> A stupid clown of the spirit's motive.[13]

His body is "a caricature, a swollen shadow, A stupid clown of the spirit's motive."

With God, this is not so. This is Saint Paul speaking in his first letter to the church in Corinth:

> Do you not know that your bodies are temples of the Holy Spirit, who is in you, whom you have received from God? You are not your own; you were bought at a price. Therefore honor God with your bodies. (1 Corinthians 6:19–20)

This is a dimension of life in God's Kingdom that we can't miss. God is everywhere in that Kingdom, into the most microscopic dimensions of cell life; his Spirit infuses every cell, every nucleus, every mytochondrium (please look up "mytochondrium" and discover the reactions that occur in one of them).

Schwartz's heavy bear is an example of how many of us divide reality into things of the body and things of the spirit. And Saint Paul himself does speak a great deal about "the flesh" and "the spirit," saying that we have to walk in the latter and not the former.

Perhaps it was as easy for people in Jesus's time as it is in ours to seize on the concrete and the material, instead of the ethereal and the spiritual. Jesus says to Thomas after His resurrection, "because you have seen me, you have believed: blessed are they who have not seen, and yet have believed" (John 20:29).

Jewish practices may be especially tactile and concrete, both centuries ago and today. When Jesus arrived, shocking things occurred that apparently required a renewing of mind before people could apprehend them, what Dallas Willard in our time calls a "renovation of the heart."

We can exchange one kingdom for another. In the passage below, C. S. Lewis says that once inside Jesus's Kingdom of God, life can be like this:

> And He and you are two things of such a kind that if you really get into any kind of touch with Him you will, in fact, be humble–delightedly humble, feeling the infinite relief of having for once got rid of all the

> silly nonsense about your own dignity which has made you restless and unhappy all your life. He is trying to make you humble in order to make this moment possible: trying to take off a lot of silly, ugly, fancy-dress in which we have all got ourselves up and are strutting about like the little idiots we are.... To get even near it, even for a moment, is like a drink of cold water to a man in a desert.[14]

The "drink of cold water" is what Jesus described to the woman at the well: "but whoever drinks the water I give him will never thirst. Indeed, the water I give him will become in him a spring of water welling up to eternal life" (John 4:14).

What Jesus was telling Nicodemus and the rich young ruler was that they needed to be reborn into a life of the spirit. When we hear this, I fear, our first response might be, "No way!" We wonder if such a life is, first of all, possible, and secondly, if it is a life we would want if we could attain it.

The Reality of Spirit

Understand, however, that we are already living the life of the spirit. Here's how Dallas Willard describes this phenomenon:

> The part of us that drives and organizes our life is not the physical. This remains true even if we deny it. You have a spirit within you and it has been formed. It has taken on a specific character. I have a spirit and it has been formed. This is true of everyone.
>
> The human spirit is an inescapable, fundamental aspect of every human being; and it takes on whichever character it has from the experiences and choices that we have lived through or made in our past. This is what it means for it to be "formed."[15]

Jesus takes this concept to a new level, in effect telling Nicodemus and others that they must be born *again* if they truly want to enter God's kingdom—exchanging, if you will, the spirits they've already "formed" (to use Willard's term) for the Holy Spirit that Jesus promises.

While we can't literally see it, we acknowledge the reality of spirit all the time. Some sports teams are said to have "fighting spirit." Those who tame horses talk of being careful not to "break" their spirit. We speak of the "letter" and the "spirit" of the law. We say that those in the grip of intense sorrow become "dispirited." Webster defines *spirit* as "an animating or vital principle held to give life to physical organisms."

So it's not that spirit isn't real, and it's not, as Willard points out, that we don't already have it. It's that for some of us, our particular spirit is not leading us toward a satisfying, peaceful, and fulfilling life, the one available to us in God's kingdom.

This is what Jesus came to provide. It is what Nicodemus needed to be born into. It is what the rich young ruler would inherit once he put down his earthly attachments. It's the "living water" leading to eternal life that he offered to the woman at the well.

To the woman at the well, remember, He said, "God is Spirit, and those who worship Him must worship in spirit and truth." Our dialogue, as it were, with God is possible largely through the medium of the spirit.

The author Stephen Covey sees spirit as our conscience. Here is how he explains God's role in it:

> I believe that correct principles are natural laws, and that God, the Creator and Father of us all, is the source of them, and also the source of our conscience. I believe that to the degree people live by this inspired conscience, they will grow to fulfill their natures; to the degree that they do not, they will not rise above the animal plane.[16]

Note in particular his use of the phrase "inspired conscience." From this inspired source comes the reminder from within that we are acting as we should.

In Dallas Willard's words:

> The revolution of Jesus is in the first place and continuously a revolution of the human heart or human spirit. It did not and does not proceed by means of the formation of social institutions and laws, the outer forms of our existence, intending that these would then impose a good order of life upon people who come under their power. Rather, his is a revolution of character, which proceeds by changing people from the inside through ongoing personal relationship to God in Christ and to one another.[17]

M. Scott Peck speaks of the final result of this revolution:

> I have said that the ultimate goal of spiritual growth is for the individual to become as one with God. It is to know with God. Since the unconscious is God all along, we may further define the goal of spiritual growth to be the attainment of godhood by the conscious self. It is to become totally, wholly God... The point is to become God while preserving consciousness... This is the meaning of our individual existence. We are born that we might become, as a conscious individual, a new life form of God.[18]

This is what Jesus calls us to be. He says, "Be perfect, therefore, as your heavenly Father is perfect" (Matthew 5:48). In the Gospel of Luke, He says, "The coming of the kingdom of God is not something that can be observed, nor will people say, 'Here it is,' or 'There it is,' because the kingdom of God is in your midst" (Luke 17:20–21). Another translation of this verse reads "the kingdom of God is within you" (NIV).

Lest you read that passage too quickly, please see that it is one important answer to the question "Where is God?" Jesus says that God's kingdom is in our midst or within each of us; M. Scott Peck says that we can become "a new life form of God." A well-known hymn's chorus is "You ask me how I know He [Jesus] lives—He lives within my heart."

The Revolutionary

If you have been picturing Jesus as the kindly Shepherd, cradling a lamb (you are the lamb), you may want to revise that picture. I said earlier that Jesus represents a shocking alternative to the lives we're living now, and let's confirm that.

Recall what happened when Jesus first called His disciples. Remember Zebedee, the father of James and John, left alone in his boat, to mend his nets and earn a livelihood on his own. His sons went off to follow Jesus.

Later, "a certain scribe" says to Jesus, "Teacher, I will follow You wherever You go," to which Jesus responds, "Foxes have dens and birds of the air have nests, but the Son of Man has no place to lay His head" (Matthew 8:19–20). Another would-be follower says to Jesus, "Lord, first let me go and bury my father." Jesus replies, "Follow Me, and let the dead bury their own dead" (Matthew 8:21–22).

Note the lack of warmth and fuzziness in the following:

> Do not suppose that I have come to bring peace to the earth. I did not come to bring peace but a sword. For I have come to turn a man against his father, a daughter against her mother, a daughter-in-law against her mother-in-law—a man's enemies will be the members of his own household. (Matthew 10:35–36)

Somehow, this part was soft-pedaled in my youthful Sunday school experiences. But don't focus simply on the relative-against-relative part. Verse 38 of Matthew 10 concludes, "Whoever loses his life for My sake will find it."

For His ministry to succeed, Jesus needed to shock His audience into wakefulness. He did this in part by the signs or miracles that Nicodemus speaks of, and He did it in part through what He said.

He needed to make it clear to His audience that life as they had been living it did not, and cannot, work. Hence His comments about the sword, about the need for us to sever ourselves from everything "in the world," including if necessary our own families, that can keep us from Him. If we can do so, He said on many occasions, great will be our rewards—here, now, and into eternity.

The Rewards

The Gospel of John begins with these words:

> In the beginning was the Word, and the Word was with God, and the Word was God. He was with God in the beginning. Through him all things were made; without him nothing was made that has been made. In him was life, and that life was the life of all mankind. The light shines in the darkness, and the darkness has not overcome it. (John 1:1–5)

John goes on to describe the role in Jesus's ministry of John the Baptist:

> There was a man sent from God whose name was John. He came as a witness to testify concerning that Light, so that all through him might believe. He himself was not the light, he came only as a witness to the light. (John 1:6–8)

And then John describes the light, and through this description, we begin perhaps to understand the rewards of a life in Christ:

> He was in the world, and though the world was made through him, the world did not recognize him. He came to that which was his own, but his own did not receive him. Yet to all who did receive him, to those

> who believed in his name, he gave the right to become children of God—children born not of natural descent, nor of human decision or a husband's will, but born of God. (John 1:10–13)

Christians believe that we are called to bring light to the world in Jesus's name. Jesus said it this way: "You are the light of the world. A town built on a hill cannot be hidden. Neither do people light a lamp and put it under a bowl. Instead they put it on its stand, and it gives light to everyone in the house. In the same way, let your light shine before others, that they may see your good deeds and glorify your Father in heaven" (Matthew 5:14–16).

Jesus's and John's use of the image of light is persuasive and compelling. (I say this as one well-schooled and experienced in the realms of darkness.) It's important for us to remember, in our roles as lights of the world, that we do not emit this life from our own power source. We can do so only if we are connected to the Source. We stay connected to Him by committing our lives to Him and by being obedient. Here is one way that Jesus describes our connection to Him:

> Come to Me, all you who are weary and burdened, and I will give you rest. Take My Yoke upon you and learn from Me, for I am gentle and humble in heart, and you will find rest for your souls. For my Yoke is easy and My burden is light. (Matthew 11:28–30)

Let me say something about being "yoked" with Jesus. It does not, at first hearing, sound like a choice for personal growth and fulfillment. That's because it isn't. It's a choice for God's kingdom, in which we are to live, not for ourselves, but to serve others (we recall Jesus saying, "The Son of Man came not to be served, but to serve").

A dramatic example of the service Jesus is talking about is His washing of the disciples' feet at the Last Supper. When He says He's going to do this, Peter, who sometimes speaks before he thinks, says, "No ... you shall never wash my feet." And tellingly, Jesus says to him, "Unless I wash you, you have no part with Me" (John 13:8).

In the kind of service that we do in Jesus's name, we are in His words the light of the world. Another of His striking images is of Himself as the "vine," and ourselves as the branches:

> I am the vine, and you are the branches. If you remain in me and I in you, you will bear much fruit; apart from me you can do nothing. If you do not remain in me, you are like a branch that is thrown away and withers; such branches are picked up, thrown into the fire and burned. If you remain in me and my words remain in you, ask whatever you wish, and it will be done for you. This is to my Father's glory, that you bear much fruit, showing yourselves to be my disciples. (John 15:5–8)

Perhaps the hardest lesson that Jesus teaches is death to self. A life of fulfillment and purpose is possible only as long as we are yoked with and grafted to Him, in the service of God and in service to other people. If we can get our minds and hearts around this idea, we might be on our way. We don't matter as individual, self-absorbed entities. We matter greatly as instruments of a larger purpose, as branches grafted to the Source.

Invitation to the Spirit

I want to conclude this chapter by referring back to the quotation with which I began it: "But when they arrest you, do not worry about what to say or how to say it. At that time you will be given what to say, for it will not be you speaking, but the Spirit of your Father speaking through you." (Matthew 10:18–20)

This reminds us that when we talk about a new, better life in Christ, we need to remember that with the coming of the Comforter or the Holy Spirit, we should come to exercise less and less control over our thoughts and actions. We are yoked, remember, with Christ. We have invited His Holy Spirit to take up residence inside us. We are conformed to Him.

Author Andrew Murray reminds us that even the disciples were relatively powerless until the Spirit descended upon them at Pentecost. Of Jesus, Murray says, "He was still nothing more than an external Christ who stood outside of them and from without sought to work on them by His word and His personal influence."[19]

But Murray says all this changed at Pentecost:

> With the advent of Pentecost this condition was entirely changed. In the Holy Spirit, He came down as the indwelling Christ to become the life of their life. He had promised this in the words, "I will not leave you comfortless: I will come to you. At that ye shall know that I am in my Father, and ye in me, and I in you."[20]

Murray goes on to say, "Only when Jesus descended into them by the Holy Spirit did they undergo a complete change. They received Him in His heavenly humility and subjection to the Father and in His self-sacrifice for others. Henceforth, all was changed."[21]

This is an important concept, one that Murray says most modern churchgoers miss: He says that most of us try to "do good works" and sincerely believe in Christ's mission. He says that we try to be responsible members of our respective congregations, but we are missing everything until we invite the Spirit of God into our lives—to live in and direct us.

Reminding us of what happened to Jesus Himself and to the apostle Paul in Damascus, Murray says we are to find someone "full of the Spirit" to lay hands on us and pray that the Holy Spirit "come into us" fully.

This is important information for those who may be rethinking their relationships with God. For most of us, attempting to shape our lives on our own has been met with checkered success. In opting for a life in Christ, we are acknowledging that we can't do it ourselves. We are acknowledging with Jesus that "with God, everything is possible."

Summary

- Jesus delivered the news to Nicodemus, the rich young ruler, and the Samaritan woman that a new reality had arrived, one that they would need to be reborn into if they were to be saved.
- In his meekness and humility, Jesus was not the warrior Messiah that the Jews expected, and they rejected His early claims to be the Chosen One.
- Life in the kingdom of God is "life in the spirit." If we are to live fully in that kingdom, we need to expand beyond boundaries of flesh and materiality in general.
- To live in the spirit, we need to acknowledge the heavy bear of our earthly embodiment and not identify exclusively with our bodies.
- We are already well-versed in the language of the spirit. We need to plug into the Light that John speaks of and allow that Light to shine through us.
- Jesus speaks of bringing not peace but a sword to earth. He needed to shock His audience into understanding the new reality represented by life in the Kingdom of God.
- We as the branches of the Tree of Life can bear much fruit (live rich, fulfilling lives obedient to Jesus's commandments), but only as long as we stay connected to Him.
- We have to ask for that connection, inviting Jesus in the Holy Spirit to enter fully into our lives and take control.

Our next chapter explores this last point in more detail. We will continue to explore what life in the Spirit means, this time as that life is revealed to us during Jesus's final days.

Chapter Six

Jesus's Final Days

Yet this is no cause for shame, because I know whom I have believed, and am convinced that he is able to guard what I have entrusted to him until that day. (2 Timothy 1:12)

Eternity

In the final days of Jesus's first earthly ministry (I say "first" earthly ministry because He promises to come again), there is considerable discussion of the final judgment, about what will happen to humankind at the end of the world, and before that, for each of us when we die. A daunting subject, for sure, but one we should probably consider. Let's at least do a kind of inventory of it before looking more closely at the final days of Jesus's first earthly mission.

There's a familiar picture of Jesus standing and cradling a lamb. The lamb is a symbol of us; He's holding each of us in His loving arms. We like this picture. Perhaps we think we've somehow earned His love and, in His arms, are right where we want and deserve to be. I know that's where *I* want to be.

While our sins are taken away by the atoning sacrifice of Jesus, according to His own words, there are still expectations of us; we can be cradled in those loving arms for a while, but perhaps not indefinitely. And if we fail in our lifetimes to meet Jesus's expectations, there are consequences. We can speculate about the kind, degree, and intensity of them, but most likely, not the fact of them.

We as His followers don't *achieve* salvation or eternal life in heaven. We are *given* salvation by grace, through the unmerited love of God through the sacrifice of His Son. Thus, while there's no earning our way into eternal life through our own good behavior, neither do we have a blank check from God guaranteeing our triumphant entry there (in effect, what we do is present "the check" written by Jesus that allows us in).

Apparently, our lives with God require both faith and a certain standard of behavior. As the book of James spells out, faith without what he calls "works" is dead. When Jesus calls us to be perfect, even as our Father in heaven is perfect, He appears to mean it.

Here is a fact from the worlds of education and business: When people direct others to do things, they rely on the clarity of instructions, followed by the administration of consequences should something remain undone. Research suggests that the former (the instruction) is a far less significant predictor of a successful outcome than the latter (the consequence). Apparently, we do what we do out of consideration of the consequences of *not* doing it.

God is a loving God, but He is also a just one, so there will be justice. Let's begin this chapter with Jesus's own words on the subject.

Sheep and Goats

Toward the end of the Gospel of Matthew, Jesus is telling His disciples about what will happen when He returns—at the so-called Second Coming. He speaks of Himself in the following passage:

> All the nations will be gathered before him, and he will separate the people one from another as a shepherd separates the sheep from the goats. He will put the sheep on his right and the goats on his left. (Matthew 25:32–33)

Jesus continues:

> Then the King will say to those on His right, "Come, you who are blessed by My Father; take your inheritance, the kingdom prepared for you since the creation of the world. For I was hungry and you gave me something to eat, I was thirsty and you gave me something to drink, I was a stranger and you invited me in." (Matthew 25:34–36)

Jesus goes on to say that even the "righteous" (the sheep) don't quite get this. They think for a moment and say basically, "We just don't remember doing this for You; when did all this happen?" Jesus answers, "The King will reply, 'Truly I tell you, whatever you did for one of the least of these brothers of mine, you did for me" (Matthew 25:40). Now Jesus's words for the goats are less friendly. To them, the King says, "Depart from Me, you cursed, into the eternal fire prepared for the devil and his angels," and He goes on to say that He was hungry and they didn't feed Him, He was thirsty and they gave Him no drink, and so on (Matthew 25:41–43).

Again His audience is kind of dim, and they say in effect, "We just don't remember *not* doing these things for You." And of course, the King replies, "Whatever you did not do for one of the least of these, you did not do it to Me" (Matthew 25:45) The goats are then sent away "into eternal punishment," and the righteous (again, these would be the sheep) go into everlasting life.

This is a throat-clearing moment in our reading of scripture.

Remember that the exchange just mentioned occurs late in Jesus's ministry. The passage above is part of the final days under consideration. Some of Jesus's audience were still not getting His message. When we distill down what Jesus is asking his followers (including us) to do in this passage, it's this:

- Give food to those who hunger.
- Give drink to those who thirst.
- Take in strangers.
- Clothe the naked.
- Visit the sick.
- Visit the imprisoned.

And we are to do all of the above for "the least" of Jesus's "brethren"—those least able to provide for themselves.

Some might think that this is a lot to ask. If you're one of those who thinks so, it gets worse, because we hear on the heels of the above what will happen if we *don't* provide for the least of Jesus's brethren. This would be the part about the punishment reserved for the devil and his angels.

Jesus asks nothing less of us than He asks of Himself: "Whoever wants to be great among you, let him be your servant, and whoever wants to be first among you must be your slave—just as the Son of Man did not come to be served, but to serve, and to give His life as a ransom for many" (Matthew 20:27–28).

Let me say a bit more about that "everlasting fire" part—the consequence of not feeding the hungry, giving drink to those who thirst, and so on. Jesus is saying through this that what we do in life matters; who we are in life matters. We either serve others or we serve ourselves. Serving ourselves and ignoring the plight of the least of our brethren—that does not speak well of us. That's going to place us with the goats of Jesus's example.

I can't consider this point, becoming a servant to others, without thinking of people like Mother Theresa, she who gave such inexhaustible service to "the least of these." Every morning on my way to work, I pass our city's homeless shelter, and I see those who've spent the night there gathered on the sidewalk. They are required to leave at that hour of the morning, and I assume that most of them have no place to go. I have to get to work, so I keep on driving. Even if I weren't going to work, I'd keep on driving.

I can't supply an excuse for this, because there isn't a reason and only the most feeble of excuses. I ask for God's forgiveness; I pray to be stronger and more giving. This response is completely inadequate. When we meet someone who's hungry, we feed them; they won't like it—and will remain hungry—if we say only "I'll pray for you."

As we contemplate the decision this book explores, to consider how we are investing ourselves, we do need to keep the sheep and goats point in mind. I agree that we do what we do in life on the basis of anticipated consequences. Maybe I should say, "I know in large part," because we also do act charitably during our best moments; we do have the ability to choose an action simply because our conscience whispers to us that it's the right thing to do. That is the Spirit guiding us.

Whatever our motivation, we need to be thinking about it right now and continuously. If we wait for a more opportune time, it may be too late. Then, as C. S. Lewis reminds us, "There is no use saying you choose to lie down when it has become impossible to stand up."[22]

The Last Supper

An important event occurs shortly before Jesus's trial and crucifixion: the Last Supper, which He shares with His disciples. The meal they share is actually the beginning of the Feast of the Passover. Passover refers to the time hundreds of years earlier when the people of Israel were still held in bondage in Egypt. You'll remember that God sent Moses and his brother Aaron to demand that Pharaoh let the people of Israel go (so they could worship Him), but Pharaoh stubbornly refused.

In response, God brought down plague after plague on the Egyptians. Do you recall them? There were the lice, the flies, the diseased livestock, the boils, the hail, the darkness, the locusts. None of these moved Pharaoh to comply with Moses's command to "let my people go."

But the tenth plague was literally a killer. God reveals that at midnight, He will go into Egypt and take the lives of all the firstborn males in the land, from children to the firstborn males of all the animals. God says, "There will be a loud wailing throughout Egypt—worse than there has ever been or ever will be again" (Exodus 11:6).

Pharaoh ignores the final warning given to him by Moses. To protect the children of Israel from the Lord (who would strike all the firstborn in the land), God instructs Moses to tell every Jewish household to select a lamb for sacrifice, one "without blemish," and put some of its blood on the doorposts of the houses where the lamb is eaten (Exodus 12:7).

God explains that the blood will be a sign to Him to "pass over" that household when He strikes Egypt with this final and most dire plague (Exodus 12:13).

The tenth plague happens as Moses warned it would. All the firstborn of the Egyptians are stricken. Pharaoh, broken at last, allows the Israelites to leave. The Passover thus becomes a feast and festival celebrated from that point forward.

This is the symbolic celebration that Jesus is to have with His disciples on the evening He arrives in Jerusalem. *He* is to be the Passover Lamb; His blood is going to save them.

That evening, Mark tells us, the following occurred:

> While they were eating, Jesus took bread, and when he had given thanks, he broke it and gave it to his disciples, saying "Take it; this is my body." Then he took a cup, and when he had given thanks, he gave it to them, and they all drank from it. "This is my blood of the covenant, which is poured out for many," he said to them. "Truly I tell you, I will not drink again from the fruit of the vine until that day when I drink it in the new kingdom of God." (Mark 14:22–25)

The New Covenant

This is extraordinary—Jesus saying that the bread is His body, the wine is His blood, and compelling His disciples to eat and drink. What did He mean? What does He mean by a "new covenant"?

Remember that in Jesus's time, the Jews were still looking for the Chosen One, the Messiah who would take them out of bondage. At the Last Supper, Jesus is reminding His disciples of the words of the prophet Jeremiah hundreds of years earlier:

> "The days are coming," declares the Lord,
> "when I will make a new covenant
> with the people of Israel
> and with the people of Judah.
> It will not be like the covenant
> I made with their ancestors
> when I took them by the hand
> to lead them out of Egypt,
> because they broke my covenant,
> though I was a husband to them,"
> declares the Lord.
> "This is the covenant I will make with the
> people of Israel
> after that time," declares the Lord,
> "I will put my law in their minds
> and write it on their hearts." (Jeremiah 31:31–33)

A new covenant was also referred to by the prophet Ezekiel. Through Ezekiel, God says:

> I will place over them one shepherd, my servant David, and he will tend them; he will tend them and be their shepherd. I the Lord will be their God, and my servant David will be prince among them. I the Lord have spoken. (Ezekiel 34:23–24)

Ezckiel continues:

> I will make a covenant of peace with them and rid the land of savage beasts so that they may live in the wilderness and sleep in the forests in safety. I will make them and the places surrounding my hill a blessing. I will send down showers in season; there

> will be showers of blessing. The trees will yield their fruit and the ground will yield its crops; the people will be secure in their land. They will know that I am the Lord, when I break the bars of their yoke and rescue them from the hands of those who enslaved them. (Ezekiel 35:25–27)

While Ezekiel refers to David (who was a shepherd in his youth), his comments reflect Jesus's references to Himself as the Good Shepherd, the one who will eventually lead God's flock to eternal life, to those "showers of blessing."

Note that Jesus Himself is saying at the Last Supper that He is the fulfillment of these and other prophecies; through His coming sacrifice, He will usher in this "covenant of peace." He is the Way that God chooses to write His new covenant in all of our hearts. Holy Communion, the sacrament that Christians observe today during which we too eat the bread and drink the wine, reminds us that this is so.

Taking the Bread and Cup

The sacrament of Holy Communion was well established in the emerging church as early as twenty-six years after Jesus's death. By that date, the church at Corinth had already begun to get the sacrament wrong and had to be admonished because of this by the apostle Paul:

> So then, when you come together, it is not the Lord's Supper you eat, for when you are eating, some of you go ahead with your own private suppers. As a result, one person remains hungry and another gets drunk. Don't you have homes to eat and drink in? Or do you despise the church of God by humiliating those who have nothing? What shall I say to you? Shall I praise you? Certainly not in this matter. (1 Corinthians 11:20–22)

This is vintage Paul: "Don't you have homes to eat and drink in?" He is never one to mince words. Don't miss His point, however. We've been discussing the Passover meal Jesus had with His disciples and the sacrament based on that which we still practice.

Paul's point is that the sacrament of Holy Communion is not a feast or a family picnic; it is a solemn re-creation of Jesus's sacrifice for them. Notice in the following passage that Paul repeats almost word-for-word Jesus's instructions to the disciples. Notice too the way that Paul learned the ritual ("I received from the Lord"):

> For I received from the Lord what I also delivered to you: The Lord Jesus, on the night he was betrayed, took bread, and when he had given thanks, he broke it and said, "This is my body which is for you; do this in remembrance of me." In the same way, after supper he took the cup saying, "This cup is the new covenant in My blood. Do this, whenever you drink it, in remembrance of me." (1 Corinthians 11:23–25)

Jesus is reminding the disciples, as Paul reminds the church at Corinth, that He is the Lamb. We recall that in the Gospel of John, John the Baptist says as he sees Jesus approaching him, "Behold! The Lamb of God who takes away the sin of the world" (John 1:29). After the Last Supper, Jesus was about to do this—take away the sin of the world—the next day.

In the Garden

After the supper in the upper room, Mark tells us that Jesus and the disciples went to the garden of Gethsemane, where Jesus leaves some of the disciples to rest and takes Peter, James, and John with Him to pray. Mark says, "He began to be deeply distressed and troubled." Then He said to them, "My soul is overwhelmed with sorrow to the point of death." He said to them, "Stay here and watch" (Mark 14:33–34).

We then read the following extraordinary passage:

> Going a little farther, he fell to the ground and prayed that if possible the hour might pass from him. "Abba, Father," he said, "everything is possible for you. Take this cup from me. Yet not what I will, but what you will." (Mark 14:35–36)

Jesus has been on an unswerving path toward this very moment. Some read this passage and say "Why, if He is the Son of God, would He be troubled—isn't He, in a real sense, above this?"

He is, of course, but He is also human, and He is facing the real human anguish that anyone would feel facing the cup that He faces at this moment. He is going to be tried, convicted, and tortured, and He will die the cruelest, most excruciating death possible. Any of us might say, "If others can do this, please let them." But notice the end of His prayer: "yet not what I will, but what You will."

Jesus prays and at intervals returns to find the disciples sleeping. To Peter, He says, "Simon ... are you asleep? Couldn't you keep watch for one hour? Watch and pray so that you will not fall into temptation. The spirit is willing, but the flesh is weak" (Mark 14:37–38).

To me, this scene in the garden illustrates the Gospels' authenticity—it sounds very much like an eyewitness account. Some maintain that since the Gospels were written well after the facts of Jesus's life and death, they were largely fabricated and embellished to aid in the establishment of the developing church. If this were so, why would the writers depict Jesus's human anguish in such detail? He asks His Father to take the cup from Him. Rather, it sounds like Mark saw Jesus in the garden, heard what He said, then recorded what He said.

Jesus is betrayed by Judas to the Jewish authorities, and we read that many "with swords and clubs" came to arrest Him. One of Jesus's followers does draw a sword and strike one of the "multitude," but Jesus tells him and the others not to resist. Jesus allows Himself to be taken because "the Scriptures must be fulfilled" (Mark 14:49).

Mark then says, "Then everyone deserted him and fled" (Mark 14:50).

To reinforce my point that an eyewitness must have recorded the events in the garden, Mark includes the following interesting passage: "A young man, wearing nothing but a linen garment, was following

Jesus. When they seized him, he fled naked, leaving his garment behind" (Mark 14:51–52).

In the first place, the pronouns in this passage are hard to unscramble. The "him" in the final sentence, we assume, is Jesus. But who is the one laid hold of? Mark could be referring to either Jesus or the young man.

But here is my question: why is this passage included at all? What does it add to the story of Jesus's last moments of freedom? It is bizarre, to say the very least. The conclusion I reach is that the reporter was there; he was trying to gather facts as best he could, and this is one fact that happened: a nearly naked man was there who lost finally his one bit of clothing and ran off.

Tradition holds that the young man is Mark himself, since his is the only Gospel that records this incident. Again, my point is that if later supporters of the church were amending the facts of Jesus's story to suit their own purposes, why would they include this part of the story? I can't believe that they would.

Death and Resurrection

Jesus's trial before the Jewish council was recounted in an earlier chapter. After Pilate reluctantly condemns Him to death, He is flogged, spat upon, given a crown of thorns to wear, and led away to be crucified. Luke tells us that Jesus's cross bears the inscription "THIS IS THE KING OF THE JEWS" (Luke 23:38).

Jesus is crucified between two criminals. Luke records Jesus saying (of those carrying out the Crucifixion), "Father, forgive them, for they do not know what they do" (Luke 23:34).

Those present mock Jesus. Some in the crowd say that since Jesus saved others, why doesn't He save Himself? The soldiers also jeer at Him, saying, "If you are the king of the Jews, save Yourself." And one of the criminals crucified with Him says, "Aren't you the Messiah? Save Yourself and us" (Luke 23:35–39).

And then this remarkable thing happens: To the criminal who asks Jesus to save them, the other criminal says, "Don't you fear God, . . .

since you are under the same sentence? We are punished justly, for we are getting what our deeds deserve. But this man has done nothing wrong." Then he said, "Jesus, remember me when you come into your kingdom" (Luke 23:40–42).

Jesus tells him, "Truly I tell you, today you will be with me in paradise" (Luke 23:43).

The criminal is dying for deeds that even he says are just cause for his punishment. And now here, in the eleventh hour of his life, Jesus is allowing him into the kingdom. Some (one thinks of the scribes and the Pharisees) would say that this isn't fair. How can several seconds of repentance replace a lifetime of sin?

An answer is suggested in a parable that Jesus told. Earlier in His ministry, Jesus spoke of workers in a vineyard. Some started work early in the morning; some came at mid-day, some not until the afternoon. In the parable, all were paid the same, and because of this, some of them complained to the landowner that they who'd worked all day were paid the same as those who'd only worked the last hour (Matthew 20:12).

But the landowner says, "Take your pay and go. I want to give the man who was hired last the same as I gave you. Don't I have the right to do what I want with my own money? Or are you envious because I am generous? So the last will be first, and the first will be last" (Matthew 20:14–16).

Those coming to faith in Christ late may well like this parable. They may conclude that they too can bide their time, perhaps thinking that they also might get an eleventh-hour reprieve when Jesus comes again. I would counsel against this thinking. The risk is too high, the probability perhaps too low that Jesus will grant to other latecomers what He grants to the thief.

Certainly, the thief on the cross was among the last, and fortunately for him, he is chosen to enter the kingdom. He makes his decision to jump onboard, as it were, as the train is leaving the station, and he is fortunate that the Conductor lets him on.

Jesus dies on the cross and is buried in the tomb of Joseph of Arimathea, as we recounted earlier. After His first appearance to the women who had gone to the tomb, He appears to the disciples on several occasions. Here is Luke's account of one of these appearances:

> While they were still talking about this, Jesus himself stood among them and said to them, "Peace be with you." They were startled and frightened, thinking they saw a ghost. He said to them, "Why are you troubled, and why do doubts arise in your minds? Look at my hands and my feet. It is I myself! Touch me and see; a ghost does not have flesh and bones, as you see I have. (Luke 24:36–39)

Jesus eats and drinks in their presence to prove that He is really there in the flesh (remember earlier comments about the disciples often failing to grasp Jesus's meanings). He reminds them, "This is what I told you while I was still with you: Everything must be fulfilled that is written about me in the Law of Moses, the Prophets and the Psalms" (Luke 24:44).

Luke then tells us, "Then he opened their minds so they might comprehend the Scriptures" (Luke 24:45).

Jesus final words to the disciples, as recorded in Luke, are:

> This is what is written: The Messiah will suffer and rise from the dead on the third day, and repentance for the forgiveness of sins will be preached in his name to all nations, beginning at Jerusalem. You are witnesses to these things. (Luke 24:46–49)

Atonement

The following could have been written after the sacrifice Jesus made for all of God's people:

> Surely he took up our pain
>   And bore our suffering,
> yet we considered him punished by God,
>   stricken by him, and afflicted.

But he was pierced for our transgressions,
he was crushed for our iniquities;
the punishment that brought us peace was
on him,
and by his wounds we are healed. (Isaiah 53:4–6)

Except this wasn't written after Jesus's death. It was written some seven centuries earlier by the prophet Isaiah in the Old Testament. These and other so-called Suffering Servant passages in Isaiah are among the clearest examples of scriptures that Jesus fulfilled through His death and resurrection. They are as well a reminder to us of the debt we owe and can't repay.

We were all bought through the sacrifice Jesus made for us. As pointed out in an earlier chapter, Paul says in his first letter to the Corinthians, "Do you not know that your bodies are temples of the Holy Spirit, who is in you, whom you have received from God? You are not your own; you were bought at a price" (1 Corinthians 6:19–20).

Max Lucado, in his book *In the Grip of Grace,* envisions a situation in which he, because he's been a negligent driver, has lost his insurance coverage. He's guilty. The insurance company has him dead to rights. The following is Lucado's hypothetical explanation of how he could once again be an insured driver. He envisions an insurance executive saying the following:

> Mr. Lucado, I have found a way to deal with your mistakes. I can't overlook them; to do so would be unjust. I can't pretend you didn't commit them; to do so would be a lie. But here is what I can do. In our records we have found a person with a spotless past. He has never broken a law. Not one violation, not one trespass, not even a parking ticket. He has volunteered to trade records with you. We will take your name and put it on his record. We will take his name and put it on yours. We will punish him for what you did. You, who did wrong, will be made right. He, who did right, will be made wrong.[23]

Lucado says that if we were to wait for an actual insurance executive to say this, we could be in for a long wait. He continues:

> But if you're wanting God to say those words, you can sigh with relief. He has. He can.... The perfect record of Jesus was given to you, and your imperfect record was given to Christ.... As a result, God's holiness is honored and his children are forgiven. By his perfect life Jesus fulfilled the commands of the law. By his death he satisfied the demands of sin. Jesus suffered not like a sinner, but as a sinner.[24]

Lucado sums it up this way: "Ponder the achievement of God. He doesn't condone our sin; nor does he compromise his standard. He doesn't ignore our rebellion; nor does he relax his standards. Rather than dismiss our sin he assumes our sin and, incredibly, sentences himself. God's holiness is honored. Our sin is punished. And we are redeemed. God is still God. The wages of sin is still death. And we are made perfect."[25]

The Wages of Sin

In the end, we all need to answer the question about life after death for ourselves. I'm a person of faith, but I don't know in the literal sense what will happen when I die. With everyone else, I have access to a lot of data on the subject, which I've certainly studied and will continue to study. But in the end, we do what we do in life based on faith. We decide who we're going to trust and believe. With Paul, I know whom I believe.

A good and enjoyable book that speaks to this issue is *The Myth of Certainty: The Reflective Christian & the Risk of Commitment,* written by Daniel Taylor.

One point that Taylor makes is simple but profound. He agrees that we can't know in any final way, but we have the capacity to commit, even in the midst of uncertainty. A simple illustration is my marriage to Marsha. I can't know enough to guarantee that we will always be together, that she will love me forever, but I know enough to commit myself in marriage to her.

St. Paul makes this point in his second letter to Timothy: "That is why I am suffering as I am. Yet this is no cause for shame, because I know whom I have believed, and am convinced that he is able to guard what I have entrusted to him until that day" (2 Timothy 1:12).

In 1883, Daniel Wittle translated Paul's idea into a well-known hymn, "I Know Whom I Have Believed":

> I know not when my Lord may come, at night or noon day fair,
> Or if I walk the vale with him, or meet him in the air.
> But I know whom I have believed, and am persuaded that he is able
> To keep that which I've committed, unto him against that day.[26]

We are now at the end of our third chapter on Jesus. We've covered the basic facts of His life; we've looked at His teaching; and in this chapter, we've examined in more detail some key events of His final days on earth. I think the Lucado illustration summarizes very well why God sent Jesus to earth.

Anne Lamont is another writer who provides a similar summary. Ms. Lamont took a rather circuitous route to God, one not unlike my own. In her book *Traveling Mercies,* she describes a time when she asked a person of faith what it meant to be saved. The person she asks is a man named Bill.

> What did it mean to be saved, I asked, although I knew the word smacked of Elmer Gantry for both of us.
> "You don't need to think about this," he said.
> "Just tell me."
> "I guess it's like discovering you're on the shelf of a pawnshop, dusty and forgotten and maybe not worth very much. But Jesus comes in and tells the

> pawnbroker, 'I'll take her place on the shelf. Let her go outside again.'"[27]

This is reminiscent of Jesus's own parable of the prodigal son. In that story, the younger of a landowner's two sons who asks for his inheritance that would eventually come to him. He gets the money, travels to a far country, and proceeds to spend it in all manner of loose living.

Destitute, he finds work herding swine, but we learn that he somehow "comes to himself" and decides that even his father's hired people live better than he is living, so he decides to return home.

He decides to return to his father, beg his forgiveness, and offer to work as one of the hired men. His father sees him coming and runs to him and embraces him, calling for the finest robe for him, a ring for his hand, and sandals for his feet. He calls for the fatted calf to be killed and a feast to be planned, "for this son of mine was dead and is alive again; he was lost and is found" (Luke 15:24).

An important point you can't miss is that this wouldn't have happened if the prodigal son hadn't *turned,* if he hadn't decided that the path he'd been on led to a life as a swineherd.

This fictional reunion of father and son is the reunion with God that Jesus makes possible. This is the reason He came, which is made especially clear through the events of His final days. But remember what the prodigal son had to do. He had to look about him, realize where he was, and turn back to his father.

In our way, each of us may be like the prodigal son. We've tried to do things our way, rarely learning in time the various errors of our ways. We read that the prodigal son "came to himself" and decided to return to his father, and maybe that's what we all need to do.

Most of us know what it's like on that shelf in the pawnshop. It may be time to ignore some of the distractions that lure us and make our way off the shelf, back into the light.

Chapter Seven

The Apostle

Join together in following my example, brothers and sisters, and just as you have us for a model, keep your eyes on those who live as we do. (Philippians 3:17)

The Inner Circle

Earlier, we talked about how Jesus picked His closest followers. There were twelve disciples. Those closest to Him were Peter, James, and John. Others are known for traits they had or positions they held. Matthew, for example, was a tax collector; Judas Iscariot managed the group's money. Jesus and his followers preached, taught, and healed the sick in the region of Galilee and beyond for some three years before His arrest and Crucifixion.

We've seen that even those in His inner circle were often slow to learn, to grasp the incredible news that Jesus brought. Peter, especially early on, was often symbolic of this difficulty in catching on. Jesus walks on the water at one point and tells Peter that he can do this as well.

Peter does so, for a few watery steps, but then sinks. Peter would say one thing—that he would follow the Master to death and beyond—but then deny three times the night Jesus was arrested that he even knew Him.

Others seem to learn more quickly, to almost intuit the deeper meaning of what Jesus said and did. Sometimes these were women. Mary Magdalene, for example, and Mary and Martha, the sisters of Lazarus, whom Jesus raised from the dead. In Mary and Martha, we see typical reactions to Who Jesus was and what He said. Mary was the intuitive one, knowing at a deep level that she must pay attention in order to appreciate Jesus's message and actions. Martha was the hands-on, industrious one. Mary would sit raptly at Jesus's feet; Martha would cook and clean.

After Jesus is crucified and rises from the dead, the apostles receive the Holy Spirit, Who empowers them to go forward and spread the good news. They do. Peter, perhaps especially, takes a lead role and brings Jesus's message courageously to those who need to hear it. While he may have been impetuous and impulsive earlier—speaking sometimes without thinking clearly—after Pentecost, he is strong, articulate, and single-minded.

The Newcomer

Jesus's immediate circle, the eleven disciples remaining after Judas's betrayal and subsequent death, were influential in spreading the news of Christ's resurrection. Peter is reborn in terms of his steadfastness, eloquence, and resolution. John, "the disciple Jesus loved," was also important, composing his own Gospel later in the development of the church, for writing his letters, and for writing Revelation, the last book of the Bible, which he composed late in life while living in exile on the island of Patmos.

But perhaps foremost among the apostles is Paul, formerly Saul of Tarsus. Let me spend a moment on Paul's background.

First, he was an infamous (at least to the emerging church) persecutor of Christians. When the first Christian martyr, Stephen, was stoned to death, Saul held the coats of those who killed him, thereby giving, if not outright approval, at least tacit acceptance of what was occurring in front of him. Some historians place Paul as a student and follower of Gamaliel, a highly respected Jewish leader and interpreter of the law, an important member of the Sanhedrin.

In earlier chapters, we talked about the Pharisees, one of several Jewish sects who were influential in Palestine during Jesus's time. The Pharisees and another sect called the Sadducees each comprised approximately half of the Sanhedrin, the council that condemned Jesus to death. They did so because He identified himself as the promised Messiah, and this they couldn't reconcile with their strict adherence to established Jewish law, as revealed in the Torah and elsewhere.

Recall comments made earlier about the immersion in their faith practiced by first-century Jews. I said before that religion for them couldn't be dabbled in. Rather, their faith was integrated into virtually everything they did and everything they considered themselves to be. And the guardians of their faith were sects such as the Pharisees and the Sadducees. We could add the Essenes to this group, an extremely conservative branch of Judaism whose members largely isolated themselves from others, the better to focus strictly on the law.

It may not be an exaggeration to think of these groups as keepers of the kingdom, often called upon to interpret specific situations and fine points of the law. Rabbis were scholars who, through rigorous study of the Torah and other sacred texts, were considered teachers and interpreters of the faith. This could be an informal designation; Nicodemus, you may recall, refers to Jesus as "Rabbi."

When we first meet Saul of Tarsus, he is deeply embedded in the Jewish religious tradition of his time. He is a Pharisee. In the Apostle Paul's letter to the Philippians, he talks about his immersion in what he calls the "flesh," those depending on circumcision and other tangible signs to demonstrate their faith, saying that that can no longer be the saving feature of religious life:

> If someone else thinks they have reasons to put confidence in the flesh, I have more: circumcised on the eighth day; of the people of Israel, of the tribe of Benjamin, a Hebrew of Hebrews; in regard to the law, a Pharisee; as for zeal, persecuting the church; as for

> legalistic righteousness, based on the law, faultless. (Philippians 3:4–6)

When he makes his comment above in Philippians, he has realized that salvation comes through faith in Christ, not through strict observance of the law.

How did this "Hebrew of Hebrews" change his thinking and his life so radically? It is among the most astonishing stories in the Bible.

The Road to Damascus

Here is how he changed.

On his way to Damascus, with orders to find and imprison more followers of Jesus, he is struck blind and hears Jesus say, "Saul, Saul, why are you persecuting me?" (Acts 9:4). And then the events ensue that I described earlier: he is sightless for three days in Damascus and neither eats nor drinks; he is baptized by Ananias (who is reluctant to do so, being familiar with Saul's history); he recovers his sight and goes on to become what Bart Ehrman describes as "the most important convert in the history of the Christian religion."[28]

Paul becomes acquainted with Peter, James, John, and the other disciples. Before Ananias baptizes him, the Lord says to Ananias, "Go! This man is my chosen instrument to proclaim my name to the Gentiles and their kings and to the people of Israel. I will show him how much he must suffer for my name" (Acts 9:15–16).

While Paul certainly preached the good news of Jesus to Jews, his ministry was also targeted to the Gentiles ("Gentiles" are those who are not Jews). It's not exactly that Paul and the disciples divided up their collective ministries, Paul to the Gentiles and Peter and the rest to the Jews, but it worked out in roughly that way.

As you might expect, given his history of persecution, the disciples initially feared Paul and were reluctant to recognize him as a follower of Jesus. As Paul began to preach, Luke tells us in Acts, "All those who heard him were astonished and asked, 'Isn't he the man who raised havoc in Jerusalem among those who call on this name? And hasn't he come here to take them as prisoner to the chief priests?'" (Acts 9:21) But Paul goes on to "confound" the Jews in Damascus, "proving that Jesus is the Messiah" (Acts 9:22).

An early convert of the disciples, Joses, was instrumental in reconciling Paul with Peter and the rest of the disciples. A Levite from Cyprus, so moved was Joses by the Gospel that he sold his land and gave the money to the apostles (Acts 5:37). Joses was renamed Barnabas (translated "Son of Encouragement") by the disciples, and he told Peter and the rest what had happened to Paul on the road to Damascus and about his subsequent ministry there.

In his second letter to the church in Corinth, Paul provides a summary of what he has been through in service to the Lord:

> Are they servants of Christ? (I am out of my mind to talk like this.) I am more. I have worked much harder, been in prison more frequently, been flogged more severely, and been exposed to death again and again. Five times I received from the Jews the forty lashes minus one. Three times I was beaten with rods, once I was pelted with stones, three times I was shipwrecked, I spent a night and a day in the open sea. I have been constantly on the move. I have been in danger from rivers, in danger from bandits, in danger from my fellow Jews, in danger from Gentiles; in danger in the city, in danger in the country, in danger at sea, and in danger from false believers. (2 Corinthians 11:23–26)

Paul doesn't talk like this very often. He, remember, is the one who is "crucified with Christ." He says that he, Paul, no longer lives, but Christ lives in him. So it's rare that he reflects on his own suffering, as he does in the passage above.

But let's not pass over this passage lightly. Five times, the Jewish authorities gave him "forty stripes minus one." By "stripe" he means wound on his back. Thus "forty stripes minus one" refers to thirty-nine lashes from some sort of whip (there were various categories of whips, and he doesn't specify which were used on him). Five times he endured this punishment. Victims of crucifixion such as Jesus were often near death before their formal executions began, because of floggings they received beforehand.

Of another occasion, Paul says only "once I was stoned." As recorded in the book of Acts:

> Then some Jews came from Antioch and Iconium and won the crowd over. They stoned Paul and dragged him outside the city, thinking he was dead. But after the disciples had gathered around him, he got up and went back into the city. The next day he and Barnabas left for Derbe. (Acts 14:19–20)

This is not Paul himself telling the story. Rather it is the historian Luke, author of the Gospel that bears his name, the one who made it a point to get all the facts right.

Three times he was shipwrecked? "A day and a night I have been in the deep"? I don't know how you read that, but I think it means he spent a day and a night *in the water.*

To return to the "perils in the sea" Paul refers to, that would be the Mediterranean Sea. Paul embarked on several missionary journeys to bring the Gospel to people throughout the eastern and northern Mediterranean, and eventually west through Crete and Malta, northward to Rome itself.

At the northern shore of the Aegean Sea (Macedonia), he established churches in Thessalonica and Philippi; along the eastern Aegean, he did the same in cities such as Ephesus and Troas. Inland, in Galatia of Asia Minor, he visited cities such as Tarsus (his birthplace), Antioch, Colosse, and Derbe. He made four missionary journeys in all, including his final trip to Rome, over a period lasting more than twenty years (from approximately 48 to 68 CE).

These were not weekend trips aboard luxury liners. His missionary trips would last for several years, and it is during these times that he would have endured his "perils in the sea." Perhaps the Mediterranean is not one of the world's great oceans, but travel on it in Paul's time, as we saw, could have its perils.

The Importance of Paul

Bart Ehrman says, "It would be easy to argue that after Jesus himself, Paul was the most important figure in the history of Christianity. It was Paul's missionary work that helped transform the followers of Jesus from a small Jewish sectarian movement in Palestine to a worldwide religion comprising both Jews and Gentiles."[29]

Ehrman goes on to say:

> It was his theological reflections on the significance of the death and resurrection of Jesus that came to form the heart of the Christian message for all time. And it was his writings that were to play such an enormous role in the canon of the new Christian Scriptures, the New Testament, of whose twenty-seven books thirteen are attributed to Paul.[30]

Important—miraculous—though his ministry was, Paul was not alone in becoming a new man in Christ. I haven't retold the story of Peter, he who was so adamant that Jesus would never wash his feet. In the garden, Peter promises that he will endure any trial for Jesus: "Lord, I am ready to go with you to prison and to death" (Luke 22:33).

And Jesus says, "I tell you Peter, before the rooster crows today you will deny three times that you know me" (Luke 22:34). And of course that's what happens. None of the disciples stand with Jesus during His arrest, trial, and Crucifixion, nor do they believe the story of the women when they first return, telling the story of the empty tomb.

But after Jesus returns, the disciples are transformed, perhaps especially Peter, who preaches forcefully after Jesus's ascension. At one point, Peter and John heal a lame man and, as a result, are called before the same Jewish High Council that had found Jesus guilty: Annas, Caiaphas, and others. These worthies ask Peter and John, "By what power or by what name did you do this?" (Acts 4:7).

Remember, Peter had three times denied Jesus the night that He was arrested, said that he never knew Him.

Now Luke tells us this:

> Then Peter, filled with the Holy Spirit, said to them, "Rulers and elders of the people! If we are being called to account today for an act of kindness to a man who was lame and are being asked how he was healed, then know this, you and all the people of Israel: It is by the name of Jesus Christ of Nazareth, whom you crucified but whom God raised from the dead, that this man stands before you healed." (Acts 4:8–12)

This is not the same man who had very recently said of Jesus "I don't know this man you're talking about" (Mark 14:71).

So we see after Jesus's return from the dead that the disciples too underwent a tremendous transformation. Peter went from cringing coward the night in the garden to the one who hurls the passage above into the teeth of those who condemned Jesus.

But Paul's conversion and subsequent career are astonishing. They are astonishing in the completeness of his transformation (from coat holder at the stoning of Stephen to a principal founder of the Christian church); in the degree and duration of suffering he endures in order to spread the Gospel; and in the wisdom, consistency, and sheer beauty of the message he carried to people about Jesus, through his New Testament letters to the Romans, Corinthians, Philippians, Galatians, and the rest.

Saul of Tarsus was transformed. He was given new life in Christ; he was "crucified with Christ," in his words, and became someone else. For those of us desirous of positive change in ourselves, he may be said to set the standard.

Paul's Message

Jesus died and rose from the dead in approximately 33 CE. Paul begins his ministry some three years later, and his first letters to the outlying churches begin in approximately 48. He continues writing those letters until approximately 70.

Paul's letters or epistles are the spiritual curriculum that he invites ("requires" is a better word) those churches to follow. The epistle considered the flagship of the letters attributed to Paul is the book of Romans, which was written in the mid-50s. In many of his letters, Paul addresses specific issues that affect individual churches; for example, his fierce letter to the Galatians, in which he takes them to task for beginning to follow what he regards as a "new" Gospel. Romans is different.

In Romans, Paul tells the complete story of Who Jesus is; what His connections are to Old Testament prophecies; how He revealed His divinity; and why, as John would put it later, He is the way, the truth, and the life.

Romans follows the book of Acts in the New Testament and begins this way:

> Paul, a servant of Christ Jesus, called to be an apostle, and set apart for the gospel of God—the gospel he promised beforehand through his prophets in the Holy Scriptures regarding his Son, who as to his earthly life was a descendant of David, and who the Spirit of holiness was appointed the son of God in power by his resurrection from the dead: Jesus Christ our Lord. Through him we received grace and apostleship to call all the Gentiles to obedience that comes from faith for his name's sake. And you also are among those Gentiles who are called to belong to Jesus Christ.
>
> To all in Rome who are loved by God and called to be his holy people:
>
> Grace and peace to you from God our Father and from the Lord Jesus Christ. (Romans 1:1–7)

This salutation reflects a pattern that Paul follows in many of the letters. You may recall from an earlier chapter a quotation from Paul in which he says, "You were bought at a price" (1 Corinthians 6:19). His salutation to the Romans reflects the fact that Paul considers himself "bought at a price"; he often refers to himself as "a bondservant of Jesus Christ."

In the line I've quoted several times already, Paul considers himself crucified with Christ. "Paul," in this sense, is dead. The only "Paul" still walking around is this "servant of Jesus Christ." He, Paul, has no other identity.

I wanted you to see the entire salutation or introduction to Romans, because in it, Paul states in his typically unflinching way exactly who he is and, lest there be any confusion, Who Jesus is. Paul wants his readers to know immediately who he is and Whom he belongs to. Remember that Jesus entered into a new covenant with His disciples at the Last Supper. In Jesus's death and resurrection, this new covenant is written on the hearts of all those who believe.

Paul makes sure in Romans that people understand this:

> But now apart from the law the righteousness of God has been made known, to which the Law and the Prophets testify. This righteousness is given through faith in Jesus Christ to all who believe. There is no difference between Jew and Gentile, for all have sinned and fall short of the glory of God, and all are justified freely by his grace through the redemption that came by Christ Jesus. God presented Christ as a sacrifice of atonement through the shedding of his blood—to be received by faith. He did this to demonstrate his righteousness, because in his forbearance he had left the sins committed beforehand unpunished—he did it to demonstrate his righteousness at the present time, so as to be just and the one who justifies those who have faith in Jesus. (Romans 3:21–26)

As we saw earlier, before the new covenant, the Jews could in effect earn righteousness (rightness) with God through adherence to the law. With the new covenant, Jesus, reflected in this passage of Paul, says that righteousness now comes through faith in Him. No other way. Faith in Him is primary. Paul will say later that the law remains important but is no longer the path to salvation; faith in Jesus is that path.

Having been "justified" through faith in Jesus, Paul tells us, "We have peace with God through our Lord Jesus Christ, through whom we have gained access by faith into this grace in which we now stand" (Romans 5:1–5).

The peace we gain through faith in Christ is gained through victory over sin. And sin, as Paul says many times, is the province of that heavy bear we alluded to in an earlier chapter. Paul says, in effect, that it's the law that in its way awakens sin: "For I would not have known what covetousness really was if the law had not said, 'You shall not covet'" (Romans 7:7).

He elaborates

> For I know that good itself does not dwell in me, that is, in my sinful nature. For I have the desire to do what is good, but I cannot carry it out. For I do not do the good I want to do, but the evil I do not want to do—this I keep on doing. Now if I do what I do not want to do, it is no longer I who do it, but it is sin living in me that does it. (Romans 7:18–20)

Remembering our earlier discussion about what parts of our being are going to lead us, Paul says, "I see another law in me, waging war against the law of my mind, and making me a prisoner of the law of sin at work within me" (Romans 7:23).

This is almost the moment. We can practically hear Paul shout, "What a wretched man I am! Who will rescue me from this body that is subject to death? Thanks be to God, who delivers me through Jesus Christ our Lord" (Romans 7:24–25). He concludes that with his mind, he is able to serve the law of God, but with his flesh, he serves the law of sin—until God saves him through Christ.

The beginning of Chapter 8 of Romans is one of the most important passages in the Bible. It is Paul's answer to the body/spirit duality that he has been wrestling with:

> Therefore, there is now no condemnation for those who are in Christ Jesus, because through Christ Jesus the law of the Spirit who gives life has set you free from

> the law of sin and death. For what the law was powerless to do because it was weakened by the flesh, God did by sending his own Son in the likeness of sinful flesh to be a sin offering. And so he condemned sin in the flesh, in order that the righteous requirement of the law might be fully met in us, who do not live according to the flesh but according to the Spirit. (Romans 8:1–4)

The law was "weak in the flesh." There is strength ("living water") in the Spirit of God through Jesus: "And if the Spirit of Him who raised Jesus from the dead is living in you, he who raised Christ from the dead will also give life to your mortal bodies because of His Spirit who lives in you" (Romans 8:11).

We shouldn't place value statements on individual passages from scripture, but if we did, we could begin with "he who raised Christ from the dead will also give life to your mortal bodies because of His spirit who dwells in you."

A moment later, he says (pay attention to the quality of this writing), "I am convinced that neither death nor life, neither angels or demons, neither the present nor the future, nor any powers, neither height nor depth, nor anything else in all creation, will be able to separate us from the love of God that is in Christ Jesus our Lord" (Romans 8:38–39).

The Love of God

As I have thought about Paul over the years, I've been astonished at his life and work. I've asked myself, "How could he do it?" The answer has to be in the passage just quoted. Nothing, to Paul, "will be able to separate us from the love of God which is in Christ Jesus our Lord."

Remember that Paul had definite anger issues. Remember from Acts how he was "still breathing threats against the disciples of the Lord." This is a significant line. His very breath consisted of threats against those who followed Jesus. But on the road to Damascus, he was struck down; he was chosen. Once he came to himself, he was a recipient of the love of God in Jesus.

Now in the letter to the Romans, he extols the virtues and the nature of love:

> Love must be sincere. Hate what is evil; cling to what is good. Be devoted to one another in love. Honor one another above yourselves. Never be lacking in zeal, but keep your spiritual fervor, serving the Lord. Be joyful in hope, patient in affliction, faithful in prayer. Share with the Lord's people who are in need. (Romans 12:9–13)

Was this the same man we heard from earlier, the holder of the coats and caster into prison of women and children? We can barely make it compute.

M. Scott Peck's definition of *love* is this: "the will to extend one's self for the purpose of nurturing one's own or another's spiritual growth."[31]

This was what Paul was doing in Jesus's name and for Jesus's sake. He saw the need for love in himself in this famous passage from First Corinthians:

> If I speak in the tongues of men or of angels, but do not have love, I am only a resounding gong or a clanging cymbal. If I have the gift of prophecy and can fathom all mysteries and all knowledge, and if I have faith that can move mountains, but do not have love, I am nothing. If I give all I possess to the poor and give over my body to hardship that I may boast, but do not have love, I gain nothing.
>
> Love is patient, love is kind. It does not envy, it does not boast, it is not proud. It does not dishonor others. It is not self-seeking, it is not easily angered, it keeps no record of wrongs. Love does not delight in evil but rejoices in the truth. It always protects, always trusts, always hopes, always perseveres. (1 Corinthians 13:1–7)

Paul gives me hope. If he can be transformed—if *he* can be transformed—then perhaps there's hope for me, indeed for all of us. He was certainly far from perfect when we first heard of him at the martyrdom of Stephen, less perfect still in his continued persecution of Jesus's followers.

And even years into his ministry, he realizes that he isn't perfect, that he doesn't see the way that Jesus would have him see. He knows that he's a work in progress. He continues his thoughts on love in First Corinthians: "Love never fails. But whether there are prophecies, they will fail; whether there are tongues, they will cease; whether there is knowledge, it will vanish away" (1 Corinthians 13:8).

And here is how he expresses his own inability to see clearly:

> For we know in part and we prophecy in part, but when completeness comes, what is in part disappears. When I was a child, I talked like a child, I thought like a child, I reasoned like a child. When I became a man, I put the ways of childhood behind me. For now we see only a reflection as in a mirror; then we shall see face to face. Now I know in part; then I shall know fully, even as I am fully known. (1 Corinthians 13:9–12)

If you're like me, you may have some childish things to put away. I hardly know where to begin.

Through the kinds of tribulations outlined at the beginning of this chapter, Paul soldiers on. Through his ministry, Paul offers himself (as Jesus ordained) as one through whom "God ... commanded light to shine out of darkness" (2 Corinthians 4:5). But he recognizes that he is only the "vessel" that Jesus envisioned—commissioned—him to be:

> But we have this treasure in jars of clay to show that this all-surpassing power is from God and not from us. We are hard pressed on every side, but not crushed; perplexed, but not in despair; persecuted, but not abandoned; struck down, but not destroyed. We always carry around in our body the death of Jesus,

> so that the life of Jesus may also be revealed in our body. For we who are alive are always being given over to death for Jesus' sake, so that his life may also be revealed in our mortal body. So then, death is at work in us, but life is at work in you. (2 Corinthians 4:7–12)

"For we who are alive are always being given over to death for Jesus' sake, so that his life may also be revealed in our mortal body." This verse is critical to understanding the priceless gift God gave each of us in Jesus, and to understanding the responsibility each of us who follows Him has in honoring that gift.

To fully appreciate what Paul is saying, we may need to first understand and then demonstrate the quality of humility. This returns us to the "death to self" discussion. As Paul did, "we" (our egotistical selves) need to get out of the way and make room for the One much more impactful in His potential to save the world.

This can be a tough lesson; if there is a tougher one, I haven't found it. Paul found it, or it found him, and we are blessed that it did.

Final Thoughts

An entire book (*The 4:8 Principle*, by Tommy Newberry) has been written on the following passage from Paul's letter to believers in Philippi:

> Finally brothers and sisters, whatever is true, whatever is noble, whatever is right, whatever is pure, whatever is lovely, whatever is admirable—if anything is excellent or praiseworthy—think about such things. Whatever you have learned or received or heard from me, or seen in me, put it into practice. And the God of peace will be with you. (Philippians 4:8–9)

And you see, we've come full circle from the quotation with which we began this chapter: "Join together in following my example, brothers and sisters, and just as you have us for a model, keep your eyes on those who live as we do." (Philippians 3:17)

Here is the remarkable thing about the passage above from Philippians. Paul isn't writing *from* Philippi. He's writing from a Roman jail, and he's chained to a Roman soldier. In this condition, he's advising us to think about whatever's true, noble, just, pure, and lovely.

Paul was finally executed in Rome for his commitment to Christ. Freed from his tribulations (though he gloried in those) and eager to finally be with his beloved Lord and Savior, we can imagine that he went to his death with anticipation.

Am I being realistic at all in holding Paul up as a model for us, here in an increasingly troubled time, some two thousand years removed from him? I am, in this way: As we just read, Paul was able to see himself completely as a vessel for God. He was crucified with Christ. What mattered was not the outer trappings of Paul but the Spirit of God in Jesus that came to shine through him.

Paradoxically, as Paul himself said on many occasions, this was a freeing factor in his life. Think about this for a moment. If we can put down our own "fancy dress," as C. S. Lewis calls it, and not worry about the impressions and contributions we make in the world, wouldn't that be a freeing thing?

Here is Paul's final word on the subject, expressed as he would say to the saints in Colosse:

> Therefore, as God's chosen people, holy and dearly loved, clothe yourselves with compassion, kindness, humility, gentleness and patience. Bear with each other and forgive one another if any of you has a grievance against someone. Forgive as the Lord forgave you. And over all these virtues put on love, which binds them all together in perfect unity. (Colossians 3:12–15)

Do you recall in Chapters 1 and 2 how we discussed the possibility of change and the difficulty of thinking clearly in today's world? Paul's world was different, but it may have been no less difficult to confront change. It was similarly difficult to clearly and methodically consider and then articulate your thoughts. Paul managed this; it's hard to imagine it being done better.

If Paul can undergo the transformation he went through, so can we. If God could work the miracles He worked through Saul of Tarsus, he can also work through us.

Chapter Eight

The Road Ahead

Do not conform to the pattern of this world, but be transformed by the renewing of your mind. Then you will be able to test and approve what God's will is—his good, pleasing and perfect will. (Romans 12:2)

The Definition of Commitment

I hope the last chapter gave you an idea as to how committed St. Paul was to his cause—spreading the good news of Jesus. His mind got radically "renewed" on the road to Damascus. From that moment forward, as you saw, Paul was all in. Toward the end of his ministry, he tells Timothy, his friend, his apprentice, and "son":

> I have fought the good fight, I have finished the race, I have kept the faith. Now there is in store for me the crown of righteousness, which the Lord, the righteous Judge, will award to me on that day—and not only to

> me, but also to all who have longed for his appearing.
> (2 Timothy 4:7–8)

Remember some of the experiences Paul had on his journeys: shipwrecked, beaten, stoned, flogged—and he never wavered. His ministry continued over two decades after his conversion. Nor was he a burden to the people he ministered to. A tentmaker, he earned money during his travels by practicing that trade. And he was a writer. He wrote the profound, beautiful, persuasive letters that bear his name in the New Testament.

It would be remarkable to endure what Paul endured at all, but to remember that his ministry lasted some twenty years makes it all the more noteworthy.

Fast-Forward

And now here we are, more than two thousand years removed from the time of Jesus and Paul. I'm going to assume that the lessons we learn from Jesus and Paul are significant for all time, both in the courage they embody and for the content of the message they communicate.

We live in a difficult time (I know; further proof of my gift for understatement). We live in a complex time, which means that it has different dimensions (e.g., political, scientific, commercial, environmental), each having the potential to affect us. We live in an especially turbulent time, politically. We are seriously impacting the environment that God provided (e.g., we now find plastic at the bottom of the oceans). We are compromising the ozone layer. Global warming is occurring at a rate faster than we assumed it would.

In our country, as I write this, many of the principles our country was founded on appear to be under siege. Hate speech has become almost the norm, a reality far from the kingdom of God with its requirement that we love one another. A tiny number of people control a disproportionate share of the world's wealth. Millions in our country live below the poverty line, as do many in the developing world. Many believe that what we have called the American Dream is only that.

In an earlier chapter, we discussed the impact of technology on all of the above. In the developed world especially, technology is almost a new religion. We require the newest, most feature-filled phones; automakers are racing to produce the first totally self-driving cars; individuals and governments compete to be the first and the most successful to conquer outer space. And speaking of outer space, apparently that too is affected by a trash problem. In our excitement to be there, we perhaps forget that spacecraft and space stations, occupied as they are by human beings, generate trash, and this trash must be managed. Apparently, we bundle it on various spacecraft, or pack it aboard other vehicles that continue in their orbits, until they re-enter our atmosphere and burn into cinders.

Remember our earlier attempts to describe ourselves as processors of all these potentially distressing phenomena. It would be difficult enough to learn and understand even the most basic aspects of modern culture (political, sociological, commercial, scientific, environmental), but we magnify the difficulty by crowding as much as we can into our mental and physical receptors. Our cups already feel full to overflowing. Like Jesus, we could well ask God to take this cup from us.

The picture of our country envisioned by our Founding Fathers requires its people to read, to think, and to deliberate. The sacrifices made by many through the years require it. A representative democracy works only with an informed (hopefully benevolent) citizenry, one concerned with the welfare of all its citizens, not simply the privileged—those with the deepest pockets and the loudest voices. Currently, we are not that. We are drowning in a stream of often profane trivia, a good bit of it coming from the highest seats of our government.

We could call this information overload, and it has two basic components. The first is volume. We attempt to process too much, and as a result overload our processing circuits. If we were businesses or factories, we'd need to put second, third, and fourth shifts to work in our processing operations to handle the volume. The second is the nature and quality of what we process. I'm sorry but it is to a large degree garbage. It is comprised of gossip, advertising, falsehoods, and content of the most trivial and prejudicial kind. The conclusions we draw from the processing we do are rarely worthy of that name.

Perhaps we need to be more selective in terms of what we allow into our consciousness. At the same time, we can't be like ostriches and stick our heads into the sand, leaving critical issues to others. With Paul, we do need to "renew our minds." We need to take Jesus as our model of "the way, the truth, and the life." That is, the method, the reality, and the life energy itself needed to confront the issues before us.

Conscious and Conscience

When I was a freshman at Arizona State University, Tommy Campbell knocked me unconscious one evening after a bout of drinking. The authorities were alerted, and a number of us were placed on disciplinary probation. I spent time in the ASU infirmary, fending off an addiction to morphine.

When I was perhaps ten years old, I knocked *myself* unconscious. I accomplished this by trying to teach myself to go off the diving board at the local YMCA. Afraid to actually bounce off the end of the board, I thought it reasonable to just run off the end of it. So I set off. But when I reached the end of the board, my feet slipped forward, and I fell backward, striking my head on the edge of the diving board before falling into the deep end of the pool. Waking up was actually kind of peaceful. I remember a feeling of gently swirling and tumbling there in the deep end of the pool. I got to the surface and saw long bamboo poles extended toward me by lifeguards. Macho guy that I was, even at that age, I waved them off and swam to the side of the pool and got in line to dive again. A girl behind me nearly fainted at the site of blood streaming down my back.

So yes, I'm familiar with the lack of consciousness. But what is consciousness itself? Dictionaries will tell us that consciousness is a state of awareness: As I write this, I'm conscious of trees blowing in the wind across the street. I'm conscious of weeds that I see in my yard, begging me to uproot them. I'm aware of those things. I can create short- and long-term memories of them. It's a dazzling feature of our mental processes that they can apprehend both current phenomena (trees and weeds), send them along neural pathways, label them, and file them away should we need them at a later time.

For considerable periods of time, neural pathways can keep us attached to incidents from the past, stored in memory. You recall from an earlier chapter the memories I have of the 1946 Chevy my dad brought home, and where I was and what I was doing when President Kennedy was assassinated.

Behaviorists theorize that we have not one but two levels of potential awareness operating. One can be called surface consciousness (or surface mind), through which we process immediate things in our environments, and the other the subconscious mind. The surface mind can be considered mission control, as we deal with our daily tasks. The subconscious mind receives, classifies, and stores information (and impressions) and also affects how we remember the number, kind, and intensity of experiences we've had in the past.

As you consider this, remember the point made above about our sheer *capacity* to process phenomena. That capacity is not limitless, and many of us are perilously close to overload. We need to keep our processing operations well-oiled and running smoothly. We can't ask too much of them. We can't waste their precious capability creating product that has no lasting value, neither to God, to ourselves, to our loved ones nor to the world at large. We must bring efficiently functioning consciousness to the world as we find it.

The Forming of the Spirit

Dallas Willard speaks of this point in detail in *Renovation of the Heart*. He does not refer to consciousness per se; he speaks about spirit. In his view, we each form our spirit at a very early age. While it seems incongruous to speak of something as intangible as spirit being "formed," apparently that's what happens as we move through life. His idea of a formed spirit impacts what I've been calling a frame of reference: it's what gives our frame of reference the "reflections as in a mirror" quality that Paul describes.

When my son David was very small, perhaps four years of age, we were looking at a house to rent or buy in a small town in Alabama. David wandered toward the fence separating the house we were looking at from the one next to it. As he approached the fence, a very large, very loud dog rushed toward the fence, barking ferociously. David was scared out of his wits. This is the kind of event that can form a spirit, in Dallas Willard's terms. David recovered quickly (or the experience receded quickly into his subconscious), but he did record that experience, first in his conscious memory, from where the emotional component of it could affect him for a time into the future, and second, into the reaches of his subconscious.

This is similar to the story told in the movie *Welcome to Marwen* that we referenced earlier, in which the protagonist's spirit was reconfigured drastically by a traumatic beating he endured. His spirit was not so much shaped as it was withered by that experience.

Individual Consciousness

Consciousness itself is not at all uniform from person to person. It is the milieu or the environment into which experience is introduced. I like the comparison to a pot of stew that each of us is continually cooking. Primary of course are the ingredients we drop into our consciousness—the phenomena that we choose to pay attention to. The ingredients and the taste of yours are much different from mine. Whatever new ingredients are dropped in both add to the flavor already there, as well as make their own contribution to the taste and texture of the whole.

If I were to continue this analogy, I would add the concept of temperature. When we add too much to the mix, and raise the temperature too high, we get mush. I perceive considerable mushiness in modern culture. I don't see a lot of what Saint Paul recommends: ". . .whatever is true, whatever is noble, whatever is right, whatever is pure, whatever is lovely, whatever is admirable. . .think about such thiings." (Philippians 4: 8)

What we say, what we think, what we feel are influenced by the environments in which we find ourselves. I think this same principle applies to the inner workings of our minds, both our surface minds and our subconscious minds. When experiences (such as the dog barking at David) intrude into these inner environments, they are welcomed or perhaps rejected by what's already in the mix, so to speak. You know the expression "It blows my mind." This is what happens when what we add to the subconscious is substantially different from what's already cooking there.

This is what makes Paul's exhortation for us to "Pray without ceasing" so shocking. For many of us, praying to God as direction and activity are substantially different flavors and textures to be adding to both our surface and subconscious minds. To continue the metaphor, the new taste may take getting used to, but the nutritional value more than compensates.

Dramatic new developments often require a paradigm shift, a radical change in the way we think about something. A paradigm is a wide, well-used neural pathway, a canal, if you will, for familiar ideas to flow through. For example, decades ago, when digital watches were introduced, we had to change our ideas about mechanical watches. The first seat belts in cars also required a paradigm shift. The Toyota Prius required one. Self-driving cars? This is not so much a shift as it is an earthquake (at least for those of us who still recall 1946 Chevies).

And of course, the paradigm shift of all paradigm shifts could be the conversion of Saul of Tarsus to the Apostle Paul—a truly earth shaking transformation.

To return to our internal processing mechanisms, this processing of phenomena is further affected by our sensory capabilities (e.g., color blindness or difficulty hearing); none of us sees, hears, touches, tastes, or smells the world in the same way. This, too, as Willard would say, can impact the forming of our different spirits. I suspect that the above applies to both surface and subconscious minds. Perhaps as memories diminish in time, while we may not be able to cite them chapter and verse, they continue to influence us in ways outside of conscious memory.

God in the Details

An article on the nature of consciousness appeared recently in *The Atlantic* written by Ross Andersen, called "What the Crow Knows."[32]

The article focuses on a religious group, the Jains (the people of the sect Andersen focuses on live in India), who believe in the sanctity of all life, human and nonhuman. They believe that all animals are conscious in a variety of ways, demonstrating many complex, even ingenious behaviors. *Mysterious* behaviors.

In Andersen's words:

> Even in a secular age, consciousness retains a mystical sheen. It is alternatively described as the last frontier of science, and as a kind of immaterial magic beyond science's reckoning. David Chalmers, one of the world's most respected philosophers on the subject, once told me that consciousness could be a fundamental feature of the universe, like space-time or energy. It might be tied to the diaphanous, indeterminate workings of the quantum world, or something nonphysical.[33]

Again: "Consciousness could be a fundamental feature of the universe, like space-time or energy."

To our current point, scientists are apparently discovering that the comments above about consciousness are true not just of *homo sapiens*, but of the animal world as well.

When I first read the passage above, I thought about the concept of the Force in the *Star Wars* movies. In the very first installment, the revered Jedi Obi Wan Kenobi cocks his head at one point, puts his hand to his forehead in clear distress, and says that he is picking up a strong disturbance in the Force. We discover that the disturbance is caused by the Empire's destruction of the planet Alderaan. Obi Wan's consciousness was attuned to the Force ("a fundamental feature of the universe").

We could theorize that the force Andersen refers to originates and operates in part at the cellular level, and we know that the processes occurring there can be examined and described in detail (in other words, they are not "diaphanous"). The processes are physical and measurable. In creation, God worked on both micro and macro levels to accomplish His purposes. We touched on this topic earlier in discussions about evolution, about what appears to be humanity's ability to adjust its DNA in response to changing environments, whether those environments are internal or external.

And yes, I know. We are some distance from God kneeling and forming Adam from the dust of the earth. But when He breathed life into Adam, He might have been providing not just the breath of life (air), but ingredients—"potentials," formulas—that would activate over time in response to changing conditions and requirements. Remember the birds and beaks we spoke of earlier.

Another Voice

In 1963, a woman named Ruby Nelson wrote a remarkable book that deals with this topic (about God working on both macro and micro levels). In *The Door of Everything,* the author assumes the role of God speaking to his people. She says at one point:

> As the great life *force* [my emphasis] expresses itself, in you or anywhere in nature, its most essential action is taking place on the microscopic level.... The activity that goes on in a realm invisible to your natural eyes is a very orderly perpetuation of chemical processes which make it possible for consciousness to experience.... In this microscopic world of cellular activity, the major work, being done at lightning fast speed, is that of tearing down various molecular substances and synthesizing new kinds to fill cellular needs.
>
> The surface mind has no idea how this work is done ... It is directed by the soul.[34]

Nelson says that there is a definite connection of the subconscious mind to the conscious mind: "They determine whether the body is a free and open outlet for the dynamic *force of life* [my emphasis], or whether only a trickle of this life force seeps through."[35]

Again from *Star Wars*, we remember Luke Skywalker having to become a "free and open outlet" of the Force in order to tap into and control its energy. In order to steer, he had to let go. Write this down: In order to steer, he had to let go.

Nelson continues:

> A turbulent surface mind, oriented around the human self, is like a dam thrown up across a river, holding back its surging waters. But a quieted surface mind, oriented only to my glory, is no longer the dam across the river but merely the banks through which the water flows.
>
> This is why the Christ message teaches that you may be transformed by the renewal of your mind.[36]

My comments a moment ago about both the content we consider in our processing centers, and the temperature at which we process it, are reflective of the "turbulent surface mind" that Nelson describes. We can choose more suitable ingredients and turn the temperature down.

Please make the connection here between St. Paul's comment on mind transformation and Willard's idea about our spirits being definitely formed. St. Paul, Willard and Nelson are talking about a definite force that acts upon us and with which our own thoughts and desires interact.

So mind, as we've come to understand it, has these two dimensions, a surface dimension and a subconscious dimension. Apparently we "live" in our surface mind, but the surface mind and the subconscious mind are connected; the pathway between the two can be widened. The flow from the subconscious one to the conscious one can be widened. The title of Nelson's book (*The Door of Everything*) expresses this idea. We need to be at work opening the door between the surface and the subconscious minds, in her words, to hear clearly what the subconscious mind (Holy Spirit) is telling us.

We remember Jesus saying to the woman at the well, "Everyone who drinks this water will be thirsty again, but whoever drinks the water I give them will never thirst. Indeed, the water I give him will become in him a spring of water welling up to eternal life" (John 4:13–14).

The "water" Jesus speaks of here is the positive flow of life energy from subconscious to conscious mind ("I am the way, the truth, and the life"). When this flow is strong enough and consistent enough, we become new creations in God, more and more like Him.

In contrast to this powerful flow, Jesus is saying to the woman at the well, in effect, "What you are consuming now, in every sense of that word, is going to dry up. What I provide is going to refresh you forever."

Rhizomes

You may be wondering what a rhizome is. Here's how Webster defines one: "A somewhat elongated, usually horizontal, subterranean plant stem that is often thickened by deposits of reserve food material, produces shoots above and roots below, and is distinguished from a true root in possessing buds, nodes, and scale-like leaves." One remarkable feature of rhizomology (my word) is its duality. Rhizomes can both reach down, root like, and they can also stretch out above, bud like.

Some, especially those schooled in psychology, see the subconscious as a kind of rhizome. Dallas Willard in *Renovation of the Heart* sees the human soul as a rhizome-like dimension through which we are connected to God. God reaches out to us through His dimension, making contact with us through our rhizome-like soul, supplying His divine nourishment to it and through it. If we were to continue with Jesus's "living water" metaphor, the rhizome image would blur into something more like a reservoir, fed eternally by the spirit, always available to refresh us.

M. Scott Peck, in *The Road Less Traveled*, has a similar idea. He says, "The development of consciousness is the development of awareness in our conscious mind along with our unconscious mind, which already possesses that knowledge."[37] Peck goes on to make this startling claim: "If you desire wisdom greater than your own, you can find it inside you. What this suggests is that the interface between God and man is at least in part the interface between our unconscious and our conscious. To put it plainly, our unconscious is God. God within us. We were part of God all the time."[38]

This is important in light of what we said several chapters ago, that it may be wise to consider the possibility of "the whole God thing." Given the idea expressed above—God residing in us as Holy Spirit from the very beginning of life—the goal may change from the discovery of God to the recognition of Him.

Conscience

There are signs that God is operative in us very early on. C. S. Lewis makes this point in *Mere Christianity.* Lewis asks us to notice in very young children that they seem to understand the concept of fairness, a sense that some things are right and others wrong. They are, in other words, moral. Where does that come from? It may be the first sign of conscience in the young person.

I'll assume that you know what I mean by conscience. We've talked about the definitions of *conscious* and *unconscious,* but not so much about *conscience.* We need to, because we've just been suggesting that God speaks to us and, as Holy Spirit, resides in us—in our subconscious mind. It could be that con*science* is one way that He articulates His ideas and desires to our conscious awareness. We may want to revisit the wisdom of the old saying, "Let your conscience be your guide."

It appears that conscience does try to influence us to do the right thing. As an example, during baseball season you might want to relax on the couch and watch the Dodgers and the Giants—but you haven't bought your spouse a Mother's Day present. You'd rather sit there in comfort, but something prods you to get up off your backside, leave the game, and go buy the present. The prodder in this example is your conscience. You didn't *have* to get the present. You may be saying, "Why can't we just go through life in neutral, not worrying about the rightness and wrongness of things?"

Well, of course, we can. However, doing so becomes increasingly uncomfortable, given the persistent urging from within, and we want to keep the world on as much of an even keel as we can (God knows there are influences enough trying to get the world to keel *over*). St. Paul reminds us that the devil is prowling around out there, "seeking whom he may devour." Not a comforting thought.

But maybe the Mother's Day present example has a much simpler explanation. There's a basic calculation involved: you want to remain in your wife's good graces; you love her. Think of the Mother's Day present as part of the normal give-and-take in a relationship. But it has wider application as well. The buying of the gift is an act of generosity; it is, in the eyes of God and society at large, a good thing, a loving thing to do. Whatever rewards or consequences may occur after the fact, so to speak, don't matter. Your buying of the gift is good. You have released some living water.

And the prompting to engage in the act came from a definite source within you. It came first from your conscience, a Resident inside you at work, trying to get you to do the right thing.

The Damascus Road Revisited

In an earlier chapter, we described the miraculous change that occurred in Saul of Tarsus while he was traveling to Damascus to throw more Christians into prison. I want you to consider this now in light of what was just said in regard to the Holy Spirit residing in each of us.

God knew what it would take to spread the good news of Jesus to a fallen and skeptical world. He knew—to again demonstrate my gift for understatement—that it would take something truly miraculous. That something was in large part the conversion of Saul and the subsequent work he undertook as the Apostle Paul.

To be sure, others were involved in spreading the good news. Others received (reactivated?) the Holy Spirit within themselves and were reborn and reanimated to near supernatural degrees; we remember the speech made by Peter to the Jewish elders shortly after Spirit life was breathed into him at Pentecost. He too became a new person.

But for energy, determination, single-mindedness, clarity, and courage, the example is Saint Paul. We read in scripture that Paul, like Jesus, performed miracles, at one point bringing a little girl back from the dead. I don't think we can quantify degrees of Spirit, but clearly God's Spirit blazed to new life in Paul, to an extent no one could have predicted.

Finding God

Paul would have been the first to say that he had found God very early in life, rather than the other way around. You recall this quotation from our last chapter:

> If someone else thinks they have reasons to put confidence in the flesh, I have more: circumcised on the eighth day; of the people of Israel, of the tribe of Benjamin, a Hebrew of Hebrews; in regard to the law, a Pharisee; as for zeal, persecuting the church; as for righteousness based on the law, faultless. (Philippians 3:4–6)

Contrast this with the passage from Galatians that I quoted earlier: "I have been crucified with Christ. It is no longer I who live, but Christ lives in me."

Many do not assist to any great extent with the planting and nurturing of the idea (and the reality) of God in their children. Rather, in our culture, we spend much time, energy, money, and emotion trying to build in them what we see as a healthy sense of themselves. We want them to develop sturdy self-concepts. We teach them that they can be anything they want to be in life. We want them to be proud of themselves.

To quite a degree, Jesus and Paul turn this thinking upside down. When Paul says "he" is crucified with Christ, he means that he, the man Paul, no longer means anything; that man doesn't exist anymore. That man is dead. Paul has achieved what some in the psychiatric community refer to as "death to self." In Jesus's speeches to the multitudes, He speaks of the first being last and the last being first; in the Sermon on the Mount, He says, "Blessed are the poor in spirit, for theirs is the kingdom of heaven" (Matthew 5:3).

Someone who is "poor in spirit" is one who has done what Paul does: dies to self in order to live for Christ.

With ourselves out of the way, we can more easily access and express the Spirit within. "We" as individuals no longer matter; we want Christ to express in and through us. Inimical to this concept is the notion of pride. Pride is one of the Seven Deadly Sins and, in the eyes of many, the father of all sin. C. S. Lewis says that compared to pride, all the other sins are "flea bites."

So perhaps our attempt to find God—within ourselves and elsewhere—is going to succeed in part to the degree that we can lose ourselves. This involves cultivating humility. To illustrate this, people may divide themselves into two types. The first enters a room and projects "Here I am!" The second enters a room and projects "There you are!" The second outlook expresses the uniqueness and value of others. The first seeks approval and attention paid to self. If you do that, stop it. You need to get out of your way.

Because when we get in our own way, we can have trouble discerning *Jesus's* way: "I am the way, the truth, and the life."

As I have rephrased that, Jesus is the method, the reality, and the life force—that spring of living water. I remember chapters ago when we visited the teenagers in *The Breakfast Club*, hearing the nerd say to the prom queen, "You're so conceited Claire; you're so full of yourself." Filled with ourselves, we may have little to no room for other things.

I want you to convince me that you get this idea—the "death to self" idea. Once concerns for ourselves are minimized, we can turn our attention to more important matters—to a fallen world that needs our attention. A difficult task? Of course, but remember the saying, "If not me, who? If not now, when?"

While this work is going on, there is other work proceeding. If we can get out of our own way; if we can become far less self-important, we can begin to discern another direction and another priority. We can begin to feel the influence of the Spirit. We can be nudged along at first but go faster as time passes, as we travel the road God has laid out for us. In the Gospel of Matthew, we hear Jesus say, "Come to me, all you who are weary and burdened, and I will give you rest. Take my yoke upon you and learn from me, for I am gentle and humble in heart, and you will find rest for your souls. For my yoke is easy and my burden is light" (Matthew 11:28–30).

You know the yoke Jesus speaks of, right? A heavy wooden contraption designed to control the movement of two oxen? Little individual movement is possible when two are yoked together. I think the image is apt. When we are yoked with Jesus, we have no choice but to go in the direction He leads us. But He says His "burden is light," and it is. Certainly lighter than the baggage most of us continue to carry—alone.

Chapter Nine

All the Right Places

I am not, in my natural state, nearly as much my own person as I like to believe: most of what I call "me" can be very easily explained. It is when I turn to Christ, when I give myself up to His Personality, that I first begin to have a real personality of my own.[39]
—C. S. Lewis

Attention Impossible

I want to return to the topic we discussed in the last chapter, this death-to-self idea. Central to it is the concept of attention: what we choose to focus on in life, and consequently, what we can choose to ignore.

For much of our lives, my oldest daughter Molly and I have not been able to spend long stretches of time together. Conscious of this, when we are together, one or the other of us will get very close to the other, look deeply into the other one's eyes, and say, "I'm going to *pay attention* to you."

In earlier chapters, I talked about distraction, about how difficult many of us find it to pay attention to virtually anything. This is a familiar example, but if you attend meetings in your working life, and you find yourself in one, look around the table and count the phones. Those are there because even in the meeting, when everyone is supposed to pay attention to the topic at hand, people are at the ready to pay attention to something else. Their phones might ring, or buzz, or chirp, or play Beethoven's Fifth—and most will feel compelled to answer them.

When television first came into our lives, we had those four channels I spoke of earlier. And if you wanted to stop paying attention to one and begin to pay attention to another, you had to get up, walk over to the television set, and manually turn a dial to change from one channel to another. Much easier to sit there and pay attention to what you'd originally chosen.

Now, not only are there hundreds of channels or stations—among which we can flick with lightning speed—but we can program the TV to record anything we may be missing and view it later. Unless, of course, we discover we don't like it, then we can flick to something else.

We have collective attention deficit disorder (ADD).

The quotation with which we began this book was Henry D. Thoreau telling us that we must learn to live more "continently," which means "deliberately." Deliberation is the antidote for ADD. It facilitates the ability to focus and concentrate. Now I'm about to make an assumption, and the assumption is this: I don't think you would have read this far if you weren't interested in our topic—about finding God, about what might be a gnawing idea that you may be missing out on something.

My conclusion about everything we've discussed so far is that if you want to find God, you're going to have to pay attention. You're going to have to look for Him, and that of necessity involves not looking for something else. Your search will have to be deliberate. Thoreau wants you to "spend one day as deliberately as Nature, and not be thrown off the track by every nutshell and mosquito's wing that falls on the rails.... Let the bells ring and the children cry."[40]

Prayer

One deliberate thing Christians do is pray. Prayer is one of those ingredients that has a dramatic effect on the subconscious mix that bubbles constantly inside us.

Prayer can seem strange to those new to Christianity. In prayer, individuals or groups say either memorized or unrehearsed things to God, requesting assistance or expressing gratitude for perceived blessings. When asked by His followers how they should pray, Jesus says this (the version that follows is from the United Methodist Hymnal):

> Our Father, who art in Heaven,
> Hallowed be thy name.
> Thy kingdom come, thy will be done,
> On earth as it is in heaven.
> Give us this day our daily bread,
> And forgive us our trespasses,
> As we forgive those who trespass against us.
> And lead us not into temptation,
> But deliver us from evil,
> For thine is the kingdom,
> And the power, and the glory,
> For ever and ever,
> Amen.

Here are key definitions and assumptions of Jesus's prayer:

- God is in a place called heaven, distinct from earth.
- God's name is sacred, holy, consecrated.
- His Kingdom is a realm in which His word (law) is primary.
- A wish is expressed that God's will be established and obeyed there.
- A request is made that God's kingdom be established on earth.
- A request is made for nourishment (daily bread, sustenance needed for life).

- A request is made for forgiveness of trespasses, sins, and wrongdoing.
- We forgive those who wrong us (those who trespass against us).
- We ask to be able to resist temptation.
- We ask to be delivered from evil.
- God is acknowledged as having power and glory eternally.
- "Amen" can be translated "So be it."

This I would call the fundamental prayer in Christianity, the distilled message that Jesus delivers on the subject.

As Jesus's most relentless and tireless disciple, St. Paul would visit a given city or area (Corinth, Thessalonica, Colosse, Philippi) and often follow up these visits with a letter to the churches there. Or he would write letters to his colleagues in the faith (e.g., Timothy and Titus), advising them of an issue they should address or simply expressing encouragement. In virtually all of these letters, he begins with an address such as the following, in which he comments on the depth and frequency of his prayers for them:

> God, whom I serve in my spirit in preaching the gospel of his Son, is my witness how constantly I remember you in my prayers at all times; and I pray that now at last by God's will the way may be opened for me to come to you. (Romans 1:9–10)

> I thank my God every time I remember you. In all my prayers for all of you, I always pray with joy because of your partnership in the gospel from the first day until now. (Philippians 1:3–5)

> We always thank God, the Father of our Lord Jesus Christ, when we pray for you, because we have heard of your faith in Christ Jesus and of the love you have for all God's people. (Colossians 1:3–4)

> We always thank God for all of you, and continually mention you in our prayers. We remember before our God and Father your work produced by faith. (1 Thessalonians 2:3)

> I thank God, whom I serve as my ancestors did, with a clear conscience, as night and day I constantly remember you in my prayers. (2 Timothy 3)

In his first letter to the church in Thessalonica, Paul also says, "Rejoice always, pray continually, give thanks in all circumstances; for this is God's will for you in Christ Jesus. Do not quench the Spirit" (1 Thessalonians 5:16–20). Note Paul's affirmation of a point made earlier, about Jesus's "living water," in his urging of his readers to "not quench the spirit."

Paul, if not "continually," prays a lot. He is the model; he's the exemplar of a life lived in and for God. As the rest of us search for God, Paul is demonstrating through prayer that it is the primary means to Him.

I discuss Paul first in regard to prayer, perhaps because I can relate to him more readily than I can to Jesus, Who also seemed to "pray continually." Jesus was often in the midst of crowds clamoring to hear him, and we read that he often found it necessary to go off by Himself afterwards and pray. Those episodes seem to recharge him, so He could recover from what had to be trying and exhausting experiences with the crowds thronging to hear Him.

On the night of His arrest, Luke tells us the following:

> Jesus went out as usual to the Mount of Olives, and His disciples followed him. On reaching the place, he said to them, "Pray that you will not fall into temptation." He withdrew about a stone's throw beyond them, knelt down and prayed. "Father, if you are willing, take this cup from me; yet not my will, but yours be done...." And being in anguish, he prayed more earnestly, and his sweat was like drops of blood falling to the ground.

> When he arose from prayer and went back to the disciples, he found them asleep, exhausted from sorrow. "Why are you sleeping?" he asked them. "Get up and pray so that you will not fall into temptation." (Luke 22:39–46)

This is the picture of Jesus I have on my wall here in my study: He is praying, looking up, hands clasped on that large rock. He is kneeling. A ray from above illuminates his head. In the background, hard to see, are several of the disciples huddled together, asleep.

Later, Jesus continues to pray, dying on the cross: "Father, forgive them, for they do not know what they are doing" (Luke 23:34). Luke records Jesus's final words on the cross this way: "Jesus called out with a loud voice, 'Father, into your hands I commit my spirit.' When he had said this, He breathed his last" (Luke 23:46).

Interchanges with God

You may be surprised to hear that I was once a teacher of English composition at both the high school and college levels. One thing I did was help people learn how to write essays. I used to refer to an essay as a "sustained utterance." When we say something, we're said to "utter" it. An essay is written to sustain a particular utterance, that is, develop an idea, often over several pages. Essay writers have an idea that they want to explicate or explain.

Writers need to be aware of three primary factors when composing an essay. These are speaker, purpose, and audience. "Speaker" refers to a reader's sense of who the writer is. Young? Old? Opinionated? Condescending? Loving? Stupid? The specific choices a writer makes in diction (word choice), paragraph development, choice of examples—all these and more factors contribute to a sense of who is speaking.

To succeed, writing must have purpose, and this must become clear to readers fairly quickly, or they will lose interest. You recall what has happened to our attention spans, to our ability to pay attention. And finally, a piece of writing must be directed to a specific audience.

A message designed for an assembly of sixth graders will necessarily differ from a paper delivered to a roomful of engineers.

In prayer, we have this three-part equation operating. You are the speaker; your purpose is to make God aware of something; and God is your audience. We said earlier that the Lord is a triune God, which means that your audience is really three in one: Father, Son, and Holy Spirit.

Consider prayer seriously as a primary way to find God; this three-part dynamic of speaker, purpose, and audience may prove useful to you if you're new to the experience of prayer.

Remember Jesus's approach as He tried to communicate with audiences. Do you recall when He told an audience early on in Nazareth that he was the fulfillment of the prophecy? That He was the Messiah? They tried to kill Him. He must have known how this particular audience would respond to Him as speaker and to His purpose. Given that purpose, He had to lay it out for that particular, hostile audience.

Let me remind you again of Jesus's parable of the prodigal son. It is instructive of the way that we all have something to turn from in order to approach God. You recall that the prodigal son was the younger of two sons asks for his share of his father's wealth, then runs off and squanders it in loose living. Standing far from home in a pig sty, he realizes that even his father's hired help are faring better than he is, so he resolves to return home.

And rather than be angry with him, his father runs to meet him, puts the finest robe on him and a ring on his finger, and orders that the fatted calf be killed for a feast and a huge celebration begun to honor his return.

Clearly, Jesus's point is that God is the father in the parable, and we are all prodigal sons returning to Him. In thinking Who the audience is for your prayers, keep this parable in mind. If you've wandered afield, if your life may not be working, God isn't going to be angry, either that you've never come to Him nor if you've wandered away—as the audience for your prayer, He's going to be delighted to hear from you.

As we saw, the prodigal son's brother is not pleased with his brother's return, and he says so to his father. You recall the father's response: "'My son,' the father said, 'you are always with me, and everything I have is yours. But we had to celebrate and be glad, because this brother of yours was dead and is alive again; he was lost and is found'" (Luke 15:31–32).

Our Father in heaven is much the same. He will be especially delighted with your purpose in praying to Him. Regardless of the content of your prayer, it is the fact of it that will delight Him, the fact that you recognize that He is the One with the potential answer to your concern; He is the home you've been looking for.

Healing

Whatever psychological profile any of us has is primarily a product of the self-talk we engage in. If we put ourselves down, if we have trouble identifying positives that we bring to others, then our psychological profile—our sense of who we are and our overall worth—is going to be fairly dismal (or a lot dismal). Self-talk happens; we talk to ourselves more than anyone else in our lives.

I say this in light of what we discussed in the last chapter. You recall the dual nature of consciousness, the fact that we interact most directly with our surface consciousness or mind, but that we can be influenced as well by messaging and emotion from our subconscious mind. You remember Ms. Nelson's book *The Door of Everything*, in which the door she references is the one between our two layers of consciousness, and our goal should be to open that door and merge the two layers. Scott Peck makes essentially the same point when he says that the subconscious is really God, that the Lord resides there for all time and is trying to break through to us.

This is Who we try to reach when we pray. Prayer is a deliberate, conscious, linguistic event, but as we engage in it, we engage the attention of the subconscious as well. We talk to God, and the calm that can ensue leads us to believe that we're heard. In part, that calm reflects the bud sprouting from the rhizome of the subconscious, working its way up toward the surface, toward that door of everything that Ms. Nelson describes.

We need to be very clear about this. The "rightest" of all the right places to find God that we speak of in our title and in our text is prayer.

Remember our interpretation of Jesus's statement "I am the way, the truth, and the life." We translated the three elements as the method, the reality, and the life force. Prayer is a primary *method*, a path to Jesus's continuing presence and influence in our lives.

The House of God

A lot of praying happens in church, one of several reasons for us to go there. In Matthew 18:20, Jesus says, "For where two or three gather in my name, there I am also." Most of the time in a church, of a Sunday morning, you'll find more than two or three. For those of us looking for God, church seems a likely place to find Him.

What is an actual church service like? In my experience, church services are usually an hour long. Here is what usually happens at our church, which happens to be Methodist: Organ music starts the service, which is a signal for the congregation to get settled and focused on what they came to do: worship God. An acolyte then lights candles at the front of the sanctuary. After this, the pastor welcomes everyone and invites people to greet one another, so everyone gets out of the pews and says, "Hello," and "Bless you," to others.

After this, the liturgist reads a selection of scripture, which the pastor will discuss during her/his sermon. "Liturgy" refers to any number of prescribed worship elements—such as reading a passage of scripture aloud—and the liturgist is designated to assist with them during the service.

A hymn is sung after the scripture reading, and then the pastor delivers the sermon or message, which usually takes twenty-five minutes. Around this point in the service, the choir sings a selection (in our church, a hand bell choir presents a selection). The offering is collected. Another hymn is sung, and any announcements are made that are necessary, usually having to do with upcoming events. Sometimes, there's a baptism, a Sunday school graduation, or similar event. A final hymn is sung, and the congregation is dismissed with a blessing.

That's it.

In church, you may experience what's called a creed. A creed is a statement of accepted belief. Our congregation often recites the Apostle's Creed. This is the so-called ecumenical version:

> I believe in God, the Father Almighty,
> Maker of Heaven and Earth.
>
> I believe in Jesus Christ, his only Son, our Lord,
> Who was conceived by the Holy Spirit,
> Born of the Virgin Mary,
> Suffered under Pontius Pilate,
> Was crucified, died, and was buried;
> He descended to the dead.
> On the third day He rose again;
> He ascended into heaven,
> Is seated at the right hand of the Father,
> And will come again to judge the quick and the dead.
>
> I believe in the Holy Spirit,
> The holy Catholic church,
> The communion of saints,
> The forgiveness of sins,
> The resurrection of the body,
> And the life everlasting.
> Amen

Not just through the reciting of the creed, but in general, we go to church to remind ourselves of what we believe. If that sounds odd or unnecessary, it shouldn't. We talked at some length earlier about ourselves as a distracted nation in a distracted world. A lot of people, events, natural disasters, wars and rumors of wars, video games, dates, phone calls, and basketball tournaments are vying for our attention. You know by this time how I feel about attention. As a generally distracted populace, we need to be reminded of the core things in life, the things we really believe in.

Remember too the processing we do in our conscious and

sub-conscious minds, how we need to be more selective in our choice of ingredients, and how we have to keep temperature at a tolerable level. Perhaps this is behind the popular choice of the word "chill." Part of me resists, however, saying that we need to "chill out" when we attend church. The traditionalist in me is too strong.

Some churchgoers complain about different aspects of church life. Why an emphasis on money? Why all the committees? Why do we have to sing that hymn so often? Why can't the pastor do more to spice up the sermon? Why does the bulletin read like a Sears Catalog? Why do I have to dress up?

While some of these ideas raise legitimate concerns, they aren't the point. We come to church with all our hopes, dreams, and fears to worship God. Church isn't another in a series of entertainments that we attend. Church isn't for the worshippers; it is for the One being worshipped.

God loves church, as do His Son and the Holy Spirit. God tunes in to church; He listens hard to those prayers. He's thrilled that you're there. In your deliberate attempts to learn more about God and perhaps develop a stronger relationship with Him, you take yourself to church to get better acquainted with Him, and to be reminded of what you believe.

Consequences

The information that follows appears in *Bringing Out the Best in People: How to Apply the Astonishing Power of Positive Reinforcement,* a book by Aubrey Daniels. He posits what he calls the ABC construct to explain why people behave as they do.

A stands for "Antecedent." Antecedents are all the things managers and parents do to elicit a desired behavior from an employee or a child. They give directions, often lengthy directions, about which there can be no confusion. B stands for Behavior. That's what happens, or fails to, after the Antecedent is explained. C stands for Consequence. A consequence is what happens if the behavior isn't carried out in accordance with the Antecedent.

The question for you is, which is more powerful as a predictor and shaper of behavior? A, the Antecedent? Or C, the Consequence? If you answered C, you are correct. Give yourself a positive consequence.

The truth of this is readily apparent. My favorite example is the warning on a pack of cigarettes, that smoking is harmful. This would be the completely useless antecedent. You never see someone look at a pack of cigarettes, recoil in horror, and say, "Whoa! I'm not smoking these."

No. The individual continues to smoke, and the reason is because of the positive consequences experienced. The consequences satisfy Daniels's criteria for predicting behavior: they are immediate, positive, and certain. What are the consequences of not smoking? They are in the future, they are negative, and they are uncertain (we'll develop a cure for cancer soon).

Christians believe in a concept called salvation. We believe that Jesus made an atoning sacrifice on the cross for all the wrongdoing done by humankind, both before and after His earthly life. Seeing Jesus approach, as reported by John in his Gospel, John the Baptist says, "Look, the Lamb of God, who takes away the sin of the world" (John 1:29). His Jewish audience would be familiar with the concept of a lamb—a pure one—offered for sacrifice.

Those who accept Jesus as Lord and Savior, the One Who died for us, inherit the Kingdom of God, both present and for all eternity. When we accept this, our sins are forgiven, and as recorded in the book of Revelation, our names are written in the Book of Life; it's as if all of our wrongdoing in this life never occurred. Jesus on the cross paid the supreme price for it. When we arrive in heaven, we will be ushered in, welcomed. As the apostle Paul says in his letter to the Romans, "You were bought at a price."

God is a loving God, but He is also a just one. From any number of situations, you can see what happens when we think we can get away with things: We continue to do them. God, in the face of all the horrible and not-so-horrible things people do, in defiance of His rules, can't simply say, "Oh, that's okay." He would not be worthy of our love and respect if He did.

C. S. Lewis has a memorable description of God's judgment. He says that God is delaying, giving us a chance, as it were, to enter the fold before it's too late. You saw a part of this quotation earlier:

> He wants to give us a chance of joining His side freely. I do not suppose that you and I would have thought much of a Frenchman who waited until the Allies were marching into Germany and then announced he was on our side. God will invade. But I wonder whether people who ask God to interfere openly and directly in our world quite realize what it will be like when He does. When that happens it is the end of the world. When the author walks on the stage the play is over.... It will be too late then to choose your side. There is no use saying you choose to lie down when it has become impossible to stand up.[41]

Jesus has paid the price for us, canceled all those tickets. We have to accept this as fact and live the lives He lays out for us.

Eternal life is the consequence of acknowledging Jesus's sacrifice for us and for living according to His commands. It is legitimate to ask, what happens if we don't?

If we follow Him by living the kind of Kingdom life He lays out, then we get to be with Him. If we don't, then we apparently choose another kingdom and another eternity. How things will be in this other kingdom, I can't say, although I will try in the following chapter.

Here is one thing that seems pretty certain to me: Earlier, I described what happened when our dog Jack died. I saw the spirit leave him. When Jesus dies, He says "Father, into your hands I commit my spirit" (Luke 23:46). Luke then tells us that Jesus "breathed his last."

Luke's words are that Jesus is "committing his spirit," by breathing his last. The breath (spirit) leaves Him and goes—where? My sense is that it doesn't somehow evaporate. You'll recall Dallas Willard's comments about our entire lives, we're "forming" our spirits. Since that's the case, it doesn't seem logical that Jesus's spirit simply gets lost in the ether. He *says* where it goes: He commits it to the Father.

And it goes to the Father in heaven. As for heaven, we have any number of speculations as to what that will be like. Regardless of which of these sounds most appealing and logical to you, we can agree that heaven's the place we most want our spirits to reside when we die. Paul lays out a thorough description of the resurrection bodies that we'll occupy when we get there, and how glorious the whole experience will be, and I trust him.

The "other place" has been described and speculated about for millennia, and we will discuss it further in the next chapter. Even if we define that place (hell) as nebulously as "apart from God," leaving out the lakes of fire and the punishment, it still seems like an ill-advised chance to take—living the kind of life that will punch our tickets to that destination. So we can make plans now to go to the other place. Jack will be there, and I'll introduce you.

Love

Several times now, we've spoken of God being the way, the truth, and the life. Keeping these three elements in mind, listen to Paul in chapter 13 of his first letter to the church in Corinth:

> And yet I will show you the most excellent *way* [my emphasis]. If I speak in the tongues of men or of tongues of angels, but do not have love, I am only a resounding gong or a clanging cymbal. If I have the gift of prophecy and can fathom all mysteries and all knowledge, and if I have a faith that can move mountains, but have not love, I am nothing. If I give all I possess to the poor and give over my body to the flames, but have not love, I am nothing. (1 Corinthians 1–3)

Jesus is asked at one point what the greatest commandment is, and He responds this way:

> "The most important one," answered Jesus, "is this: 'Hear, O Israel: The Lord our God, the Lord is one. Love the Lord your God with all your heart and with all your soul and with all your mind and with all your strength.' The second is this: 'Love your neighbor as

> yourself.' There is no commandment greater than these." (Mark 12:28–31)

This is from John:

> Dear friends, let us love one another, for love comes from God. Everyone who loves has been born of God and knows God. Whoever does not love does not know God, because God is love ... since God so loved us, we also ought to love one another. No one has ever seen God; but if we love one another, God lives in us and His love is made complete in us. (1 John 4:7, 11–12)

We spoke earlier about God in both micro and macro form. He is in the midst of cell chemistry, making sure all those reactions occur on schedule. He can make fine adjustments to our DNA. He is also the sum of the parts. In Jesus's words, He is the vine, and we are the branches. Life force itself flows only from Him into each of us.

Remembering what we said earlier about God in the subconscious, we realize His presence most strongly when, through conscious effort, we are able to attract His Spirit through the door of everything, making sure it permeates the total fabric of our lives and thoughts. This is how Jesus's spring of living water is enabled to flow most freely. The water itself is God's ever-replenished, inexhaustible love for us.

We *find* God in large part through our individual capacity and potential to love. This book explores finding and discovering God, and He's been with us and in us all the while. Finding Him, however, is only the first step in sustaining His kingdom here and now. The next steps involve enlarging the capacity and potential to love that we each possess.

What the World Needs Now

Allen Skorpen said something really hurtful to me when we were in the ninth grade. Al was my best friend, which made what he said even more hurtful. He said, "Jim, you're interested in the care and feeding of Jim Hall."

He might as well have added, "And nothing else."

The fact that what he said was correct didn't lessen the hurt. The fact that what he said in large part is still true continues to convict me.

I was, and am, selfish. Self-ish. My care and feeding continue to be of the utmost importance to me. One small, saving grace I may have is that I know these things are true of me, and this knowledge can be the beginning of change. I'm saddened that my selfishness affects my family, my friends, my workmates, the people in my church. I am easily hurt, and I hold onto hurts tightly. Among the most unloving things human beings do is close off those who have—or who we imagine have—hurt us. My word for this is "freezing." I withdraw.

Perhaps this wouldn't convict me with so much force if I had more time and if the world didn't need so badly for me *not* to withdraw. Instead of withdrawing, I need to forgive real or imagined hurts, and engage with the world and those in it. I need to be more loving and forgiving. Those of us in the faith tend to say that line of the Lord's Prayer a bit too swiftly and unselfconsciously: "as we forgive those who trespass against us." Peter asks Jesus at one point, "Lord, how many times shall I forgive my brother when he sins against me? Up to seven times?" Jesus responds, "I tell you, not seven times, but seventy-seven times" (Matthew 18:21).

We don't do this. We hold onto the hurts. I've held on to Allen's comment now for decades.

That stew we're continually cooking in our subconscious? Add love. Add prayer. I would say "Season to taste," but if you add these last two ingredients, little else may be needed.

In closing this chapter, I have some favors to ask:

- Remember what's at stake as you contemplate life with or without God. You are at stake, and you will be for a long time.
- Be conscious of the effects of distraction. The planet needs our directed attention; we need as much focus and attention as we can muster. We don't need brief dollops of positive, directed

activity in service to the planet and its environment; we need a lot of it.

- Engage with people without the aid of electronic devices. Look at them and talk to them.
- Recognize and work on your capacity to think.
- Go to church. Realize Who lives there, and don't be critical.
- Become more familiar with the Bible.
- We must all try to get over ourselves and look to the needs of others.
- Develop humility.

Here's C. S. Lewis's last word on that subject:

> Look for yourself, and you will find in the long run only hatred, loneliness despair, rage, ruin and decay. But look for Christ and you will find Him, and with Him everything else thrown in.[42]

Our pastors would say of Lewis's final point, "Amen, and amen."

Chapter Ten

Full Circle

> Let us settle ourselves, and work through the mud and slush of opinion, and prejudice, and tradition, and delusion ... till we come to a hard bottom and rocks in place, which we can call reality, and say, This is, and no mistake.[43]
>
> —Henry David Thoreau

Great thinkers through time have concluded that human life must have meaning. Thoreau in the quotation above suggests that it's best if life's meaning is not mere "mud and slush," but something with a "hard bottom and rocks in place."

Some people have meaning articulated to them early in life. I envy those children whose parents instilled in them clear direction and values from the beginning. Such children had at least a framework upon which they could hang the events of their lives. They had models in their parents of what a life lived within that framework looked and felt like. They learned the meaning of love and felt the sustaining power that love can provide. If their parents loved them, why then, they must be creatures of considerable value.

My brother Bob and I had absolutely no doubt that our parents loved us, and I'm endlessly grateful for that. It's interesting that neither of them, neither Larry nor Agnes, was effectively parented. Larry, my father, shouldn't have been the oldest child in his family, but he became that when his older brother Leroy was given an incorrect prescription and died at age four. My grandmother never recovered from that, and poor Larry was the one who tried to behave himself into something he could never become.

My mother's mother Helen died when she was eight. Agnes had three sisters and a brother, and she was the third oldest, behind Clara and Edna. Theirs was a religious, churchgoing family. Not their father, Einar, but the church decided that the children would be separated and distributed among families of the congregation after Helen died, and so they were. Agnes was basically indentured to another family, one whose matriarch was not unreservedly kind and loving to her.

So my parents certainly didn't know their Dr. Spock when my brother Bob and I began our life journeys with them. What we did know, because Agnes and Larry told us and showed us, was that they loved us.

So we're launched into life in wildly different ways, with wildly differing crew people aboard with us, and we somehow have to find our way. Life presents itself to us, and we have to figure it out and move ahead—or not. Sometimes, we run in place; other times, we flounder.

You can probably anticipate what's coming: Jesus said, "I am the way, the truth, and the life." In this final chapter, I want to discuss some lingering issues you may have, some things you still may be sorting out, before you step—even tentatively—into a life with Him.

You Bet Your Life

Most of us learn way later than we'd like how brief our lives are. The teenage years, the young adult years—during these times, we think our lives will go on forever, and they don't. This is reflected in the way many in our culture prepare for retirement: They don't! One statistic indicates that 57 percent of people in America have less than a thousand dollars in savings accounts. And experts say that $1 million in savings (or investments) at age sixty-five will not last thirty years. Read into this what you will, but one conclusion seems to be a "live for today and the devil take the hindmost" approach.

Eating, drinking, and making merry may well satisfy for a moment, but only for a moment. Also, if we're not careful, the devil may take the front most along with the hindmost. I'm blessed that my youngest daughter Annie always grasped this point—about not thinking first and foremost about eating, drinking and making merry. I believe Annie still has the first coin she ever received—I think it's a 1947 Indian Head Nickel.

But let's leave Annie stacking her coins, and return to a point made in earlier chapters. We talked about the pace of modern life, about how difficult it seems to be for us to give life's issues the attention and intentionality they require. We talked about how social media and technology may be keeping us perpetually distracted. So I get it: thinking hard and systematically about the future is a tall order right now, but one that we ignore at considerable cost. And perhaps we may need to rethink and redefine "future": it ticks away, one second at a time, so what we do, right now, matters.

Here's what I want to do, and I hope you'll sit still for it. At this point in my life, I personally have decided that Christianity is reality. It embodies an approach to life that is more beneficial to me personally and to life at large than other explanations. In this closing chapter, I want to anticipate questions and issues you may have and provide my responses to them. I understand that I'm not an authority. There's a saying that describes what a believing Christian might say to one who is new to faith: "Christianity is one beggar telling another where he found bread."

So, from one beggar, on to these issues and questions.

The universe is so vast, there are galaxies bumping into other galaxies, stretching out light-year after light-year; how can Christians say that here on one little dust speck of a planet, the Creator of the Universe decided to conduct His experiment, creating and then living with human beings?

I have a lot trouble trying to understand this dust speck that I'm living on, to say nothing of understanding the vastness of the universe as a whole. Second, I only know the mind and activity of God through what has been revealed in His own words and through the words of others who've written about and experienced Him here on earth. And, I've had experiences of a more direct nature with God and Jesus.

C. S. Lewis anticipated a similar question, but one focused on life here on our planet. What should we think about earthly civilizations who've never considered the God of Abraham, Isaac, and Jacob? Those whom the Gospel has never reached? Are we to throw them into hell, simply because they haven't yet received the Word? Lewis says, "God has not told us what His arrangements about the other people are. We do know that no man can be saved except through Christ; we do not know that only those who know Him can be saved through Him."[44]

Paul and others in scripture address this issue. In a discussion of the new covenant in Christ, he anticipates questions about those who have no knowledge or experience with it. He says of those whose thought life and behavior match those of the new law, that they in effect comprise a law onto themselves. I believe Paul would say that they are welcome in the Kingdom of God. His words are, "Indeed, when Gentiles, who do not have the law, do by nature things required by the law, they are a law for themselves, even though they do not have the law. They show that the requirements of the law are written on their hearts" (Romans 2:14–15).

We don't yet know what's written on the hearts of the Martians and the Venusians out there in our solar system, nor on the hearts of those living in galaxies far, far away.

As John and other writers in the Bible describe, God is Spirit. Isn't it asking a lot for us to acknowledge, let alone worship, something we can't see?

Part of my answer to this has to do with electricity. I can't see it. I can see wires, cords, and outlets, but I can't see electrical current itself. Electricity is nonetheless real. To cite another example, when I look down at my forearm now, there is current pulsing through it as well.

There is a force behind that pulse. We can't always see with our eyes that which "pulses" this way and that in our lives.

We have the description in Genesis about God creating Adam in His own image. Also in Genesis, we read that God enjoys walking in the garden in the cool of the day. We could conclude that since Adam was a man, created in God's image, that God must be man-like.

In scripture, we have Jesus explaining to His followers that if they've seen Him, they've seen the Father. Thus, it's safe to conclude that God can be a human being if He chooses to be. In scripture, He also speaks to Moses from a burning bush. He leads the Israelites in the Exodus from Egypt in a cloud by day and in a pillar of fire by night, the better to guide them on their way. He assumes the shape He needs to accomplish a specific purpose at a particular moment in time.

You may be familiar with the word *avatar.* In the sense that I'll use the term, an avatar is a manifestation of something: it is the embodiment of something that is by nature *disembodied*. God in human form as Jesus of Nazareth can be considered in this way: He (Jesus) is "Emmanuel," or "God with us."

Several times in earlier chapters, I quoted Jesus as saying, "I am the way, the truth, and the life." It's the last word of these three that can be difficult to explain. On the one hand, Jesus may be saying, "Mine is the life I have in mind for you"; in other words, "I want you to live like Me." But we can also take this much more literally. When Jesus breathed His last on the cross, he said, "Father, into your hands I commit my spirit" (Luke 23:46).

We can interpret this as Jesus saying, "I am literally life itself." "Spirit" can thus be understood as the amalgam of all those factors/qualities/essences that constitute life. When newborn babies first gulp in air and begin to wail (while their internal life, absorbed in the womb, is still functioning), their earthly life begins with that first inhalation. It ended for Jesus when He breathed it out, surrendered it, to His Father.

When we see life—in trees, animals, birds, human beings—in my mind we see God. Jesus allowed us to see God "fully fledged," if you will, as a human being.

The disciple Thomas said that he personally would believe only what he could see and touch. In response to this Jesus said "Because you have seen me, you have believed; blessed are those who have not seen and yet have believed" (John 22: 29).

But this is a truly seminal question; in its way it's at the heart of any faith walk a person may have—belief that something is so, even though we can't see it, describe it, measure it. When we take communion in church, one of the last things the congregation says is, "As we proclaim the mystery of faith." We do know the Creator through that which He has created, and through the iteration of Himself that He has given us in Christ.

Christians talk about a personal relationship with Jesus. What's that all about? How is a personal relationship possible with someone who died a long time ago?

Think about books that you've read; they can be fiction, biography, history, virtually any genre. Especially if the book was particularly long, you develop a fairly deep knowledge of the characters: how they talk, how they think, how they act, how they relate to others, what they believe in, and so on. After you finish the book, the characters live on in your memory.

This is what happens when you read the Gospel accounts of Jesus's life in Matthew, Mark, Luke, and John. It's what happens when you hear interpretations of Jesus's life and message from those who were closest to Him, such as Peter and John. It's especially true of the one who was struck blind by Him on the Damascus Road, Saul of Tarsus. You hear what Jesus says in many different situations; you see what He does, how He interacts with many different kinds of people. You hear the astounding message that He brings.

You won't believe this until you experience it, but you will never encounter another person—in real life, in books, in movies, on television, in public office, or in any other setting—who will affect you the way Jesus does. I have been deeply affected this way. I am certainly no more insightful, educated, intelligent, perceptive, or sensitive than anyone else (in fact, I'm toward the back of the pack), but I have the concrete evidence of my experience, plus the vicarious experiences

I've had through books and other works of art. I've gathered my impressions of Jesus and I hold them close. I know Him from His words and through what he did as revealed in the scriptures, and I know the direct, personal comfort He's given me when I've needed Him.

There's an old saying, "You don't know that Jesus is all you need until Jesus is all you have." Experiencing Jesus as someone I've had with me in a dark moment is another reason I know it's possible to have a personal relationship with Him. In that moment He was all I had, and He was sufficient. Through His presence darkness can lift and light return.

There's a popular hymn about Jesus in the Methodist Hymnal titled "He Lives." A line in that hymn is "You ask me how I know he lives? He lives within my heart."

As another Person in the triune God comprised of Father, Son, and Holy Spirit, those of us who believe carry in us the Holy Spirit as well, the One Jesus refers to as the Comforter.

Noah and the Flood; Shadrach, Meshach, and Abednego in the fiery furnace; Moses parting the Red Sea; Jonah in the belly of the whale; Elijah killing hundreds of Baal's prophets; David killing Goliath with a slingshot—can we really believe what we're asked to believe in the Bible?

When we look at the Bible, we are advised to look at it all of a piece, which means that we don't cherry-pick whole books or individual verses or specific stories and say, "I believe this one is true, but I don't believe that one is true."

In fact, truth or verisimilitude (the appearance or likelihood that something is true) may not be a fair standard to apply to parts of the Bible. The Bible contains psalms (poems or songs); it contains the Song of Solomon, which is an extended love song; it contains proverbs, often brief statements written to communicate basic pieces of God's advice; it contains histories and prophecies. We take from all of these forms and genres the elemental truths about God and human life that their authors were trying to convey.

This is not to say that we can't verify the historical accuracy of much that is in the Old and New Testaments. We can match the prophecies of Isaiah and Jeremiah to the reigns of historical kings, down to the specific years those reigns begin and end. We know that Daniel served in the court of Nebuchadnezzar in Babylon after the fall of Jerusalem, rising to the position of prime minister.

When we come to the Gospels of the New Testament, we discover documents unlike any we may have ever seen before. The synoptic Gospels of Mathew, Mark, and Luke are accounts of Jesus's life and ministry, which we explored in some detail earlier. They contain character, plot, and dialogue, which can make them more accessible to modern readers. The Gospel of John is more discursive, which means that it is not bound by a strict chronology but delves perhaps more deeply into Jesus's divine nature, revealed especially through John's lengthy re-creations of Jesus's sermons.

The Bible is an artistic, historical, and theological treasure, as Jesus's disciple John would say, "full of grace and truth." Look at it and appreciate it in all of these contexts.

When doctors perform an autopsy, do they find something in the body called a soul? If not, what are we to make of the Bible's frequent references to the human soul?

The human body, in any given moment, is a miraculous symphony of processes, transmissions, reactions, and impulses, all proceeding from organs and tissues and chemicals combining to produce thought, emotion, and action. How are all of these combined within our bodies to enable us to think and act and feel as we do? That would take a far more patient, knowledgeable, and robust mind than mine to understand and explain.

We all have some rudimentary knowledge of the human brain; is the brain the same thing as the soul? I'm inclined to say no. I would be hard put to describe the brain's simplest-to-understand functions (receiving and classifying sensory information, for example), let alone more complex operations such as signaling individual muscles how to respond to given situations. How, for example, does a baseball player hit a 97 mph fastball? Think of that situation for just a moment: what would be involved in the brain's processing of the specific situation (the score in the game, the tendencies of the opposing pitcher, the signals from the third base coach)? How would the result of all that reading culminate in a decision to swing at or take a pitch?

As complex and impressive as brain activity is, does that complexity result in the creation and operation of a soul? Something for certain has to perform the coordinating and decision-making function—something, as it were, that is greater than the sum of its parts. Dallas Willard actually diagrams all this in concentric circles, depicting a center as our heart or spirit; a circle encompassing that as our mind; another that he calls "social"; and the extreme outer circle, meaning that it influences all the preceding circles, which he characterizes as soul.[45]

Helpful as that diagram may be, the reality of soul can still be elusive. We sometimes refer to an individual person as a soul, and this makes sense when we think of the soul as the center, the control room of the individual, the issuer, as it were, of the last word on a given topic. Maybe "governing principle" is a good way to characterize soul.

Now what the soul incorporates as it carries out its decision-making functions can also take direction from outside itself. Dallas Willard refers to it as having a semi-permeable membrane (a barrier that allows some entities or particles from without to pass through it), and this semi-permeable quality enables it to receive direction from outside (from God, in Willard's view[46]). You may want to refer back to the discussion of rhizomes in Chapter 8 for more on this topic. A bottom line may be that the soul is the interface between our subconscious mind and God.

The title of this book is *Finding God.* I have two questions: what makes you think some people have lost Him? And please say again where and how we can find Him.

Moses brought God's Ten Commandments down from the mountain to the people of Israel. Those commandments are pretty basic descriptors of desirable human behavior. We have no other gods than God; we honor our parents; we don't covet (yearn for) things that belong to others; we don't kill; we don't steal; we don't lie; we don't commit adultery; we remember the Sabbath; we don't swear falsely.

If we tune in to the world around us today, do we see lying? Stealing? Adultery? Swearing? Do we see what amounts to the worship of other things? Such as status or money? I think we could compile a pretty long list of anti-commandments. My assumption is that if people were walking with God (reading the Bible, praying, engaging in service to others, denying themselves), we would have a different kind of world. We would have what Jesus calls the Kingdom of God.

For that kingdom to come alive in a vibrant way, we would have to, as Paul says, "put on the mind of Christ." In modern life, we see the putting on of ideas that are a far cry from those of Christ. This is why I've recommended finding God. Maybe I should add, "Or rediscovering Him."

To quite a degree, we become what we pay attention to. Stephen Covey says that many of us develop specific "centers," becoming absorbed with one, often to the exclusion of others.[47] We can become centered on money, work, possessions, pleasure, friends, enemies, church, self, spouse, or family. I'd add technology to this list. The point is, an over-involvement with any item on this list leads to lack of involvement in another.

I believe many have lost God, often because they've found too many other things to occupy their time and attention.

We talked earlier about where God is to be found. Most prominently, He is the animating Spirit of life, that current that we spoke of earlier. He is what left Jack that day on the veterinarian's table. God is the Operator Who oversees all the interrelated organs and systems that work cooperatively in our bodies to give each of us life. He can operate inside and outside of natural law, independently of it when necessary. This is what Jesus, God with us, did when He performed His miracles: turning the water into wine, healing the sick, casting out demons, raising the dead.

In truth, He is easy to find, in that He is everywhere. He is everywhere that life is; in addition to the way and the truth, He *is* the life.

Can we review again how we get to heaven instead of the other place?

As someone perhaps new to the faith, you may be unfamiliar with the term *evangelism*. This word refers to attempts by people in the faith to explain the Gospel to people unfamiliar with it. The Gospel, or good news, of Jesus is that He died for our sins. Once we acknowledge Him as Lord and Savior, we are saved. In an earlier chapter, I spoke of the Book of Life, which includes the names of all those entitled to eternal life in heaven. Once our names are inscribed there, all records of sinful behavior that could have been used to condemn us are wiped clean, expunged. This can happen, as it were, in the eleventh hour of our lives. It did, you recall, for the one thief on the cross, the one who asks Jesus to remember him when He comes into His kingdom. Jesus said to him, "Today you will be with me in paradise" (Luke 23:43).

Evangelists can get something of an unfavorable reputation; they can be seen as pushing people to make commitments they're not ready to make. I would try to be patient with them if you happen to feel that way, because they understand what's at stake in asking you to make a commitment to Christ. If they do seem pushy, remember they're considering the vastness of eternity. I can stand the shot of Novocain at the dentist's because I know the pain is going to be momentary; successive Novocain shots stretching beyond the horizon would be a different matter.

I haven't said a lot in this book about the devil (the Director of the Other Place), but I believe that he's here in our dimension. Jesus and Paul are certainly convinced of this. It's interesting that when we get closest to God, we're mostly likely to be attacked. I remember the physical sensation of losing my breath and my balance in the midst of a spiritual activity, almost falling down. I don't have an alternative explanation other than the attack was the work of the Old Other One.

I like what C. S. Lewis says about the devil: "I know someone will ask me, 'Do you really mean, at this time of day, to re-introduce our old friend the devil—hoofs, horns and all?' Well, what the time of day has to do with it I do not know. And I am not particular about the hoofs and horns. But in other respects my answer is 'Yes, I do.' I do not claim to know anything about his personal appearance. If anybody really wants to know him better I would say to that person, 'Don't worry. If you really want to, you will. Whether you'll like it when you do is another question.'"[48]

I don't want any of us to take the idea of hell lightly, but neither do I think it's a place of burning lakes of fire and perpetual torment. In his book *The Case for Faith*,[49] Lee Strobel interviews J. P. Moreland, an acknowledged authority on the nature of heaven and hell, the author of a book entitled *Beyond Death: Exploring the Evidence for Immortality.*

Moreland rejects the idea that God condemns people to everlasting torment, but Strobel reports that Moreland does have another view of hell. This is Moreland speaking: "He [God] has made us with free will and he has made us for a purpose: to relate lovingly to him and to others. We are not accidents, we're not modified monkeys, we're not random mistakes. And if we fail over and over again to live for the purposes for which we were made ... then God will have absolutely no choice but to give us what we've asked for all along in our lives, which is separation from him."[50]

We are to "relate lovingly to him [God] and to others." That's what we have to do; that's why we were created; that's what all of our intricate engineering was designed to carry out. We have free will, and we can choose not to be loving, but if we spend a lifetime being unloving, then that will be our lot forever. Perhaps no lakes of fire or pitchforks, but unutterable sorrow over how different things could have been. According to Moreland, that's what hell is.

What is the evidence that you find most persuasive for the facts of Jesus's life and ministry?

There are several things.

First, Jesus Christ rose from the dead. Those who say He didn't are obliged then to say what *did* happen after He was crucified, dead and buried. People have been trying for hundreds of years to provide other explanations for what happened, and they haven't been able to. Here is what St. Paul says about Jesus's resurrection:

> But if it is preached that Christ has been raised from the dead, how can some of you say that there is no resurrection of the dead? If there is no resurrection of the dead, then not even Christ has been raised. And if Christ has not been raised, our preaching is useless, and so is your faith (I Corinthians 15:12-14)

In addition to the fact that He rose from the dead, another persuasive factor for me is that the documents included in the New Testament were written so soon after the events they record happened. Some people believe these documents have been altered through the centuries to align more closely to the religious agendas of different individuals and organizations. For example, the Gospels could have been edited to make the disciples appear more steadfast and devout. I see no evidence that this happened. Again, the closer to an event that a document is written, preserved, and disseminated, the more likely that document is to be accurate and trustworthy. The Gospels and other books of the New Testament have been dated to decades and less from the events described in them. For more on this topic, read Chapter 3 of Strobel's *The Case for Christ*, "The Documentary Evidence."[51]

A third factor that strikes me is the change that occurred in Jesus's disciples after His resurrection. Remember that all of the disciples deserted Him after His trial and punishment. Once Jesus returns to them, risen from the dead, they are transformed, taking the good news to the world, even in the face of torture and death. They accepted the potential consequences and kept moving forward. Another who exemplifies this dramatically is Paul. It is almost inconceivable that he went from his Pharisaic roots to one who was "crucified with Christ."

And fourth, as mentioned earlier, is the uniqueness of Jesus. I've met a lot of people; I've traveled the United States. I've read about a lot of people, and in life, in history, and in art, I've never found anyone like Jesus. He is unearthly. It's interesting to watch Him in scripture trying to get His disciples and others to see the points He's trying to make. He's a Stranger in a strange land, the Monarch of a realm that the world has never seen before.

He comprises for us the foundation, the "hard bottom and rocks in place" that Thoreau describes at the beginning of this chapter.

I will leave you with some final words of Daniel Taylor; they are from his book *The Myth of Certainty*:

> I believe the reflective Christian I have described in this book can be one who is totally committed to being an instrument of God's grace to a wounded world ... while the life of faith will never be safe, it can be secure. Faith may lead us into all kinds of dangers—physical, intellectual, and spiritual—but it simultaneously gives that sense of meaning and purpose to life that is the groundwork of security. I do not expect to leave this life with all my doubts resolved; I do hope to leave it in good standing with Him from whom all meaning flows.[52]

This is a hope that I share, and one that I wish for you.

Afterword

If you've ever moved, do you recall that last phase, going through the old house with a box, broom, and dustpan, making sure you've taken care of everything? Well, here I am, dustpan in hand.

Our title is *Finding God,* and I needed to find God in my life because I hadn't found sufficient meaning elsewhere. I looked in all the wrong places. Remember the saying from earlier, "You don't know that Jesus is all you need until Jesus is all you have"? That realization came home to me in a way that nothing else had ("I am the way, the truth and the life").

I learned that we can't dabble in matters of faith. Sooner or later we have to decide. For me it occurred in the early morning hours, in a motel room in Columbus, Mississippi. I was turning "the whole God thing" over and over in my mind, until I finally said, "Okay: You've got me." He received me (I think He already had) and He hasn't let go.

I don't know if you've been on a similar journey. I don't know if you have peace and the ability to sleep through the night. I don't know if you have love and friendship in your life. But know this. A life with God is not like a vacation or a trip to the store. He will *expect* things of you! You will need to give Him the place in your life He's been asking for, the place He deserves.

This idea flies in the face of many of our cultural norms. As a people, we are, to a degree I've never seen before, *self*-absorbed. Driving home tonight (it could be any night), I pulled up beside a car that was waiting for the light. The driver was staring at her phone, which was perhaps ten inches from her face. She was not absorbed in the task at hand; she was distracted, pulled away from something important that was asking for her attention (this would be driving).

I think we do this in dozens of ways, every day. We're looking and looking and looking, but I don't think we're finding. What we do find is not what we hoped it would be.

No, from my perspective, creation is not heading in the direction God planned for it. It's for us, His agents in this dimension, to help Him do something about that. Is that a daunting task? Of course it is, but who, remember, is going to tackle it if we don't? Once again, "If not me, who? If not now, when?"

We need to pay attention and think better. You'll remember earlier discussions about knowing what our words mean. We have to care for and preserve our nation. Right now, we aren't doing so. In terms of individual access to the basics of life, too many lack that access. While we can say, "Grab those bootstraps and pull yourself up," that's hard when people lack boots, and when their experience has taught them that the only direction available to them is down.

Jesus's words that convict me in this area are "As you've done for the least of these, you've done for me." You'll remember my blithe passing of the homeless people on my way to work.

God is all powerful, but we shouldn't make His tasks harder than they need to be. He's there, listening and waiting. He's ready with His training program. When we graduate, we can sing, "I know whom I have believed, and am persuaded, that He is able, to keep that which I've *committed*, unto Him, against that day."

Like Robert Frost,

> I have promises to keep,
> And miles to go before I sleep,
> And miles to go before I sleep.

I pray that I keep my promises, Help God with His, and travel far before I sleep.

Jim Hall
Hanover, Pennsylvania, November 2020

Bibliography

Allen, David. *Getting Things Done: The Art of Stress-Free Productivity.* New York: Penguin Books, 2001.

Anderson, Ross. "What the Crow Knows." *The Atlantic* 323, no. 2 (March 2019): 38–49.

Covey, Stephen R. *The 7 Habits of Highly Successful People.* New York: Free Press, 1998.

Ehrman, Bart. *Peter, Paul and Mary Magdalene: Followers of Jesus in History and Legend.* New York: Oxford University Press, 2006.

Hamer, Dean. *The God Gene.* New York: Doubleday, 2004.

Lamont, Anne. *Traveling Mercies.* New York: Anchor, 2000.

Lewis, C. S. *Mere Christianity.* New York: Touchstone, 1980.

Lucado, Max. *In the Grip of Grace.* Dallas: Word Publishing, 1996.

Murray, Andrew. *Experiencing the Holy Spirit.* New Kensington, PA: Whitaker House, 1985.

Nelson, Ruby. *The Door of Everything.* Marina Del Rey, CA: DeVorss & Company, 1963.

Peck, M. Scott. *The Road Less Traveled.* New York: Touchstone, 2003.

Piper, Don, with Cecil Murphey. *90 Minutes in Heaven: A True Story of Life and Death*. Grand Rapids, MI: Revell, 2015.

Schaff, Philip. "Quotes: Jesus' Influence on History." Glenham Baptist Church, June 29, 2019.

Schwartz, Delmore. *Selected Poems (1938–1958): Summer Knowledge*. New York: New Directions Publishing, 1967.

Strobel, Lee. *The Case for Christ*. Grand Rapids, MI: Zondervan Publishing House, 1998.

Strobel, Lee. *The Case for Faith*. Grand Rapids, MI: Zondervan Publishing House, 2000.

Taylor, Daniel. *The Myth of Certainty*. Downer's Grove, IL: Intervarsity Press, 1992.

Thoreau, Henry David. *Walden, or Life in the Woods*. New York: Signet Classic, 1999.

United Methodist Hymnal. Nashville: Abingdon Press, 1989.

Willard, Dallas. *Renovation of the Heart*. Colorado Springs, CO: NavPress, 2002.

Endnotes

1 Henry David Thoreau, *Thoreau on Man & Nature* (Mount Vernon, NY: Peter Pauper Press, 1960), chapter 4.

2 Henry David Thoreau, *Walden: Or Life in the Woods* (New York: Signet Classic, 1999), 72.

3 Dallas Willard, Renovation of the Heart (Colorado Springs: Navpress, 2002). 51.

4 Don Piper with Cecil Murphey, *90 Minutes in Heaven: A True Story of Life and Death* (Grand Rapids, MI), 43–44.

5 Thoreau, *Walden*, 5.

6 Daniel Taylor, *The Myth of Certainty: The Reflective Christian & the Risk of Commitment* (Downer's Grove, IL: Intervarsity Press, 1992), 21–22.

7 David Allen, *Getting Things Done: The Art of Stress-Free Productivity* (New York: Penguin Books, 2001), 12–13.

8 Dean Hamer, *The God Gene* (New York: Doubleday, 2004), 6.

9 Hamer, *The God Gene*, 6.

10 C. S. Lewis, *Mere Christianity* (New York: Touchstone, 1990), 153.

11 Lewis, *Mere Christianity*, 153.

12 Philip Schaff, "Quotes: Jesus' Influence on History," Glenham Baptist Church.

13 Delmore Schwartz, *Selected Poems (1938–1958): Summer Knowledge* (New York: New Directions Publishing).

14 Lewis, *Mere Christianity*, 114.

15 Dallas Willard, *Renovation of the Heart* (Colorado Springs: Navpress, 2002), 13.

16 Stephen Covey, *The 7 Habits of Highly Effective People* (New York: Free Press, 1998), 319.

17 Willard, *Renovation of the Heart*, 15.

18 M. Scott Peck, *The Road Less Traveled* (New York: Touchstone, 2003), 282–83.

19 Andrew Murray, *Experiencing the Holy Spirit* (New Kensington, PA: Whitaker House), 22.

20 Murray, *Experiencing the Holy Spirit,* 22.
21 Murray, *Experiencing the Holy Spirit,* 23.
22 Lewis, *Mere Christianity,* 66.
23 Max Lucado, *In the Grip of Grace* (Dallas: Word Publishing, 1996), 74.
24 Lucado, *In the Grip of Grace,* 75.
25 Lucado, *In the Grip of Grace,* 75.
26 *United Methodist Hymnal* (Nashville: Abingdon Press, 1989), 714.
27 Anne Lamont, *Traveling Mercies* (New York: Anchor, 2000), 43.
28 Bart Ehrman, *Peter, Paul and Mary Magdalene: The Followers of Jesus in History and Legend* (New York: Oxford University Press, 2006), 101.
29 Ehrman, *Peter, Paul and Mary Magdalene,* 122.
30 Ehrman, *Peter, Paul and Mary Magdalene,* 122.
31 Scott Peck. *The Road Less Traveled,* 81.
32 Ross Anderson, "What the Crow Knows," *The Atlantic* 323, no. 2 (March 2019), 39.
33 Anderson, "What the Crow Knows," 40.
34 Ruby Nelson, *The Door of Everything* (Marina Del Rey, CA: DeVorss & Company, 1963), 78–79.
35 Nelson, *The Door of Everything,* 79.
36 Nelson. *The Door of Everything,* 79.
37 Scott Peck, *The Road Less Traveled,* 280.
38 Peck, *The Road Less Traveled,* 281.
39 Lewis, *Mere Christianity,* 190.
40 Thoreau, *Walden,* 191.
41 Lewis, *Mere Christianity,* 66.
42 Lewis, *Mere Christianity,* 191.
43 Thoreau, *Walden,* 78.
44 Lewis, *Mere Christianity,* 65.
45 Willard, *Renovation of the Heart,* 38.
46 Willard, *Renovation of the Heart,* 39.
47 Covey, *The 7 Habits of Highly Effective People,* 119–21.
48 Lewis, *Mere Christianity,* 51.
49 Lee Strobel, *The Case for Faith* (Grand Rapids, MI: Zondervan Publishing House, 2000), 171.
50 Strobel, *The Case for Faith,* 173.
51 Strobel, *The Case for Christ,* 70.
52 Taylor, *The Myth of Certainty,* 153.

Printed in the United States
By Bookmasters